There

for a lief

For there is hope for a tree,
if it be cut down, that it will sprout again
and that its shoots will not cease.
Though its root grow old in the ground,
yet at the scent of water, it will bud
and put forth branches like a young plant.

JOB 14:7–9

There Is Hope
for a Tree

Pauline O'Regan

Margaret – It's been
a joy to meet you.
Come back! Love –
Pauline O'Regan RSM
(9 · 7 · 01)

AUCKLAND UNIVERSITY PRESS
BRIDGET WILLIAMS BOOKS

First published 1995
Auckland University Press with Bridget Williams Books
University of Auckland
Private Bag 92019
Auckland

ISBN 1 86940 132 8

Cover design: Mission Hall
Cover illustration: *Tree*, 1943, watercolour by Rita Angus
Rita Angus Loan Collection
Museum of New Zealand Te Papa Tongarewa
Reproduced with permission of the artist's estate

Set in Berkeley by Auckland University Press
Printed in Wellington by GP Print

To my nieces and nephews

Margaret & John, Mary & Acky, Mary & Paul,
Mary Jane & Peter, Nicky & Mark, Terry, Josie & Gary,
Trish, Carmel, Mary & Graham, Jo-ann & Vince

with love and delight in their friendship

Contents

Introduction *1*

1 Beginning Again *3*

2 An Old Man in a Hurry *8*

3 Into the Light *11*

4 Monastic Life Again *16*

5 Pain and Paradox *19*

6 The Challenge of Change *25*

7 Ireland *33*

8 The Myth of the 'Other' *45*

9 The Other's Shoes *51*

10 Where to Start? *56*

11 Making History *64*

12 Ten Years On *71*

13 The Beginning of Siege *76*

14 Are Popes Always Right? *84*

15 Dilemma and Decision *93*

16 Nevertheless It Does Move *104*

17 Looking Two Ways at Once *113*

18 Crisis of Obedience — Or Crisis of Authority? *119*

19 I'm Sorry, Ladies, to Be So Late *127*

20 She Looks Like Christ *135*

Conclusion *142*

Introduction

In many ways this book has written itself. Certainly it made its own decision about the contents! Over the past few years I have kept writing, keeping my hand in as it were, not sure where I was going. I was well started on this enjoyable exercise when the book that was emerging began to ask for something more serious and I felt I had no option but to agree, albeit reluctantly. The result is a combination of storytelling and religious reflection. The book, which begins in 1979, the year I travelled overseas on a Winston Churchill Fellowship, claims its coherence from the intertwining threads of that experience of travel on the one hand, and on the other, from some reflection triggered by certain memorable aspects of that experience.

Not everyone will agree with all I have written, but fortunately friends can disagree and friendship still survive. My hope is that this book will speak to those who have left the Catholic church and have found no other spiritual home. May they take heart from these pages and perhaps gain a new perspective on their situation.

This book may well be of interest, too, to people who have never belonged to the Catholic church. It should, at least, help them to come to some understanding of people in their lives who are Catholic and who are struggling to find their spiritual moorings in a church that is in the midst of a great struggle of its own. Catholics no longer have the luxury of the old certainties that all but robbed them of their need for faith. They are having to discern what can fruitfully be changed in the teaching of the church and what is abidingly changeless. They are experiencing all the risk entailed in following Christ in the context of the modern world.

1

It is my dear hope, too, that those who have remained in the church and who long for it to take them more seriously as loyal and perceptive adults living their lives in the reality of the modern world will find some encouragement in these pages. They have gifts of faith, awareness and understanding that they long to share with the church, but so often they do not find it listening. Even when they have a good experience in their parish life, they find that church policy emanates from an often autocratic and remote centralised source. More than anyone else, these are the people who have prompted me to write this book. I thank them for the encouragement, for the discussions and for the necessary lubrication of many cups of coffee. They are dear friends and I hate to see them despondent.

There will be many others whom I don't know but who will perhaps identify with what I have written. I'd like them to feel that they have met another pilgrim along the way who understands what they are feeling. They need to remind themselves that the church has a great need of them. In God's good providence, they could well be its scent of water.

1 Beginning Again

I made the decision to retire from teaching quite suddenly. And the driver of a delivery truck, whose name I don't know, played a vital part in bringing me to that turning point in my life. I will always be grateful to him.

One warm summer's afternoon near the end of 1977, I was sitting at the back of the hall at Aranui High School, one of the supervisors for an examination. The hall was packed with fifth form students, row on row of them, doing a dry run for School Certificate, which was due to begin in a few weeks' time. I was looking at their backs, pondering what the history students from my class were writing for me to read. Some of them had done no serious study for the whole year. Not that they had been idle. They'd worked in dairies for up to five hours after school, they'd surfed over at Taylor's Mistake, they'd delivered papers, they'd done milk rounds, they'd carried out important personal research on the opposite sex at the local mall or even in the Square and they'd done any number of other educative things of far greater interest to them than the causes of the Second World War. But on this hot afternoon in this examination room, not even the most experienced outsider could have assessed which ones knew what they were writing about, and which ones didn't. Everyone was writing — furiously, page after page. Face-saving is not the preserve of Eastern cultures only.

In the midst of all my rumination a delivery man came to the big glass doors at the back of the hall. He was looking for the office. The quickest way was across the back of the hall, a route he could have taken without anyone being remotely aware of his presence, least of all the heavy-breathing writers bent over their desks. Looking across at him just as he caught

3

sight of the rows of students, I picked up the look of startlement and awe on his face. Suddenly I was struck by the enormous gap between what he perceived as the importance of what was going on and my own perception of it, and I began a frenzy of beckoning and mime to persuade him to come on through. I couldn't bear to see him struggling off with a huge carton on a hot day, trying to find another way to the office. I mimed that nothing of any real moment was going on, that most of them were probably writing rubbish anyway, that there was no other quick route to the office, that he must not take all this so seriously, that he was too important to be tiring himself out unnecessarily. Marcel Marceau could not have done better. But it was all to no avail.

As he turned away, shaking his head at me and evincing signs of regret that teachers were not vetted more closely, I sat nursing my disappointment, reflecting on how people in general and parents in particular find it so hard to come to a school and feel at all familiar with or at ease in its environment. But most of all, I thought about that delivery man and how overwhelmed he had been by the sight of that examination room, and of his diffidence about, even reverence for, what was going on there. I set out to analyse why he took it all so seriously while I did not take it seriously enough. I was completely chastened when I placed his obvious respect for what went on in schools beside my apparent lack of respect. There had to be a reason. And there was. I had simply been there too long.

While the exam continued on its way, I took out a pen and paper and did a résumé of my life. I sat in shocked disbelief as I gazed at the outline of the years and realised that, since the age of five, I had spent only three of the following fifty years outside a classroom. I had a year at home after I left school rather prematurely, I came back home for a year after my mother died, and one year of my novitiate in the convent had been what was known as a canonical year, a time given completely to spiritual formation. Every succeeding year since then, I had gone into a classroom at the beginning of February and walked out of it in early December. School was the air I breathed. I was at ease in every aspect of its life: the play-ground, the staffroom, the classroom, the library, the examina-tion room. I enjoyed every moment of it, that paradoxical mix of security and challenge, of the expected and the unexpected, of routine and surprise. And if the ordered structure of school life provided the security, the expected, the routine, it was the young people coming in with each new year who brought with them the challenge, the unexpected, the surprise. But, enjoy it or not, I decided then and there that it was enough. I would finish at the end of the year.

Suddenly the dry run for School Certificate became a very special occasion. It was all happening right here in this room and I felt a wave of loss for the humanity and familiarity of it all. As I heard the desperate, last-minute rustling of papers I knew with complete certainty that some would have done all sixteen questions where only eight were required, that some would have done both the 'either' and the 'or' of optional questions, that some would have acted as if there were no questions at all and written everything they knew anyway, and that some would be handing in the near-perfect paper. I felt overwhelmed with affection, hope and understanding for each one of them.

That night I shared the whole experience with my commu-nity and the next day went to tell Arch Gilchrist, the principal, of my decision. Arch had no idea that I had been planning to retire, but then neither had I until the day before. He paid me the compliment of trying to dissuade me and, had I been less certain, he would undoubtedly have shaken my resolve. After five years at Aranui High School, I knew him more as a friend than a principal and I respected his judgment, with good rea-son. But not this time. When he saw that I had made up my mind, he resorted to good advice. He had known teachers who had taught over a lifetime and, when they stopped without any preparation, had suffered heart attacks. He thought it would be unwise to go straight into a new kind of work immediately. I should give myself a break of some kind — I should go for a trip overseas!

One day he sat beside me as we each ate our lunches in the staffroom. He'd thought of the perfect solution. I was to apply for a Churchill Fellowship. Until that moment I had never heard of such a thing but Arch, with his irrepressible enthusiasm, said, 'You apply, Pauline, and I'll be your referee and you'll get one.' And the upshot was that I did, and he was, and I did!

So the beginning of 1979 found me preparing to go overseas to study programmes of community development in England, Ireland, Scotland and certain places in the United States on the way home. It was an over-ambitious itinerary, all to be done in the space of three months on a very small budget. And I did it all, and wrote it up in great detail for the Churchill Memorial Trust Board on my return. What I didn't tell them was that I came home completely worn out and covered in shingles. But I brought home much more than shingles. As time went by, I realised I had some marvellous memories that were only incidental to the various programmes that I saw in Brixton and Birmingham, in Leicester and Edinburgh, in Dublin and Glasgow.

I doubt if I would have survived if I had travelled alone. But I was lucky to find two wonderful travelling companions — a friend, Lorraine Clancy, and the local Presbyterian minister, Donald Malloch. The latter is a man of many parts. A fourth-generation Southland farmer of Scottish descent, Donald had been called by God to be a minister in his church and had left his farm, gone to Knox College and was now ministering to us all in Aranui. His pastoral care reached far beyond his own church and he had become an integral and much-loved part of the wider community. Intensely interested in all forms of community development, he had shown a lively and good-humoured envy of my plans to visit community-based programmes in so many different places. When he heard that Lorraine was coming, he decided that it would not be inappropriate for him to join the party and take an overdue sabbatical break. We were an odd trio. But it turned out to be a great success. The three of us sat in on every interview and it soon became apparent that most people found Lorraine by far the most interesting member of the party. Men, particularly, tended to address everything to her. It may have had to do with her obvious interest in everything and it may have had to do with her being the youngest and the best-looking, but it took a load off me. It meant that I could listen without having to take the responsibility for every response. As for Donald, he had mastered the art of self-effacement for so long that he now practised it with consummate ease. As a result, he took in more than either Lorraine or I and amazed us afterwards with the details that we had missed. It was a very satisfactory arrangement and when I came to write my report I realised that I had doubled my knowledge and my experience by having such company.

2 *An Old Man in a Hurry*

L ike most newcomers to the world of travel, I had no idea what an exhausting enterprise it can be. As a result, I planned an itinerary that would have challenged the resources of a woman half my age. I enthusiastically studied community projects in Brixton, Birmingham, Leicester and Edinburgh without any break in between, getting as many viewpoints as possible about each one and writing notes far into the night. My batteries were running very low when, before we left Scotland, we prepared to attend a week-long seminar given by Charles Elliot, whose challenging books on development were well known to us. This was to take place on the island of Iona in the Hebrides off the coast of Northern Scotland.

Reluctantly, I have to admit that at this stage of my life I knew virtually nothing about Iona. For me, the holy places of the Western world had to be such centres of pilgrimage as Assisi in Italy, Lourdes in France, Fatima in Portugal, Knock in Ireland and Compostela in Spain. It appeared entirely natural to me that such places were not only holy but Catholic! No one had told me about Iona.

The curtain-raiser for this memorable visit took the form of a meeting with the man who, more than anyone else, had been responsible for the restoration of Iona as a place of pilgrimage. George McLeod had been a Presbyterian minister in Glasgow during the worst days of the Great Depression and all around him he saw the evil of grinding poverty destroying the lives of unemployed people. While they were without work, they were without hope. In response to this tragic situation he conceived of a project that would provide employment for hundreds of people and, at the same time, engage them in an inspiring and ennobling enterprise. He himself would lead them to the island of Iona and work with them in restoring the abbey that had been in ruins for centuries.

Iona had been in the hands of clan Campbell since the year 1695, but in 1899 the eighth Duke of Argyll had given the island, with its sacred history and its ancient ruins, into the hands of the Church of Scotland. In 1910, St Mary's Cathedral, which was an integral part of the abbey, had been completely restored, but the abbey itself still lay in ruins beside it. So it was that in 1938, under the inspiration of George McLeod and with help from many different countries of the world, the newly founded Iona Community undertook the work that would restore the abbey and its cathedral to their original form. Once again they became the focal point of Iona, just as they had been fourteen centuries before when pilgrims had flocked there from all over Europe.

It was a privilege to meet George McLeod, who was then over ninety years of age. Donald Malloch had long been a keen admirer and the two men had corresponded over the years. On this account he received us at his Edinburgh home with the utmost warmth and pleasure. He was a distinguished-looking man whose upright carriage and lively stance belied his age. He wanted to know all about our lives and work in New Zealand and expressed a great interest in our experiences since coming to Britain. It was obvious that his passion for justice was undiminished and he questioned us closely about those places where we had seen a spirit of community being fostered and new avenues for employment opening up. But it soon became apparent that the fire of his spirit now had almost a single focus — disarmament. After a lifetime of striving to help build a better world, he had come to see that the world itself was in mortal danger through the threat of nuclear war. There was only one sure way to prevent such a cataclysm: to get rid of all the instruments of war. The nations must agree to disarm. Although in 1979 in Britain this was not a popular stance, there was nothing he would not do to spread the gospel of disarmament: he gave public lectures, wrote articles, lobbied governments around the world, corresponded internationally with like-minded people and talked of little else to those whom he met.

At one point he went to his desk and gave each of us a copy of a speech he was going to deliver in the House of Lords the following week. In his role as Baron McLeod of Fuinary he attacked the complacency of the Lords on every possible occasion. It was a speech full of facts and fire, well researched, passionate rather than emotive. I tried to imagine his voice ringing out its contemporary warning around that ancient chamber. He brought to my mind the words applied to Gladstone when, still prime minister in advanced years, he tried in 1893 to get an act through the British Parliament that would give Ireland the right to a parliament of its own. (That was the same year that the New Zealand Parliament was giving women the vote!) Gladstone was unsuccessful and his opponents dismissively termed him 'an old man in a hurry'. And here, it seemed to me, was yet another old man in a hurry, also trying to fend off future disaster and, once again, no one wanted to hear.

3 Into the Light

To get to Iona we travelled by car to the port of Oban on the west coast of Scotland and caught a ferry there for the island of Mull. I remember very little about this trip except that I was already bone weary and it did nothing to allay my tiredness. The bus that carried us from one side of Mull to the other was of vintage class and the trip across the barren island on a narrow road took some two hours. It was not a comfortable journey and it was a dull, overcast day into the bargain. We arrived finally at Fionnphort, the port of Mull, and caught the waiting boat for Iona. It was only a matter of minutes before we saw the dark silhouette of the abbey and, because it was so unexpected, it took us a few minutes more to realise that it was set in sunlight. In a ten-minute trip we passed from one world to another, from darkness to light.

Later, when we remarked on this to the local people, they told us that one of the remarkable things about Iona is that it has a lot more sunshine than even its nearest neighbours. As on this particular day, the clouds can be brooding over nearby Mull while, ten minutes away, the sun is shining on Iona. Archaeologists have provided an ancient testimony to this phenomenon with evidence that the sun-worshipping Druids adopted Iona as a centre of religion in pre-Christian times. It would seem that these early mystics sensed something unique in the atmosphere of the island, some quality that nourished the spiritual life, long before Saint Columba set foot on its shores.

It would take a long time, perhaps a lifetime, to discern all the things that make Iona so special, but one that is immediately discernible is the sparkling clarity of its light, which

11

seemed to define its environment in an extraordinary way, intensely sharp but with no element of harshness. It had all the crispness of light that we are familiar with in New Zealand, but there was also a golden quality that gave it a strange softness.

Iona is a tiny island, 5.5 kilometres long and 2.5 kilometres broad. The beauty of the place is breathtaking. It was autumn when we were there and the hay was heaped in miniature stacks in the fields surrounding the monastery, the gold of the harvest reaching right down to the incredible blue of the sea. I had seen all these colours in landscapes at home, but never quite like this. It was their intensity that was so arresting: the golden-green that is peculiar to autumn, the fruit red on the trees, the brightness of wild flowers, yellow, blue and scarlet against the grey stone cottages and the sombre darkness of the abbey, all enveloped in the warm glow of an afternoon sun. And from the first moment we had the sense of stillness and peace that is the hallmark of Iona, acknowledged by all the pilgrims who go there. I found it almost eerie at first, encountering it after a period of frantic activity, but gradually it seeped into my body, dispelling every feeling of tiredness and haste and preoccupation with getting things done. On Iona, time stands still.

For all that, the spiritual quality of the place goes much deeper than its beauty and peace. I believe that any building which has known life for a long time and which has sheltered its inhabitants through the sorrows and joys of daily living, absorbs the spirit of those people in its walls. In my own life I am grateful that, at seventy-three years of age, I can still return to the house in which I was reared. Each time I go home I have the experience of entering the presence of my parents and my sister and brother and sister-in-law and little niece, all of whom lived there before they died. There is no sense of seance about this, just a matter-of-fact awareness that, while they are always close, in this place their presence becomes part of my reality. I don't believe that it is just a case of heightened memory, although that must play a part. I think it comes from another level of consciousness where the spirit has greater freedom and deeper knowing. And, because I was not a stranger to this fusion of past and present, I was better able to recognise what happens to virtually everyone who comes to Iona.

The Christian history of Iona began in the year 563. That was the year that Saint Columba and his twelve followers landed their coracle on the south coast of this island at what is still known as Port a' Churaish, the port of the coracle. Columba was born on 7 December 521 in Donegal, during that golden age when Ireland was renowned everywhere as 'the land of saints and scholars'. Because he was born of a royal family he had access to the best learning of the time. He attended a monastic school at Moville, near Belfast, and was the pupil of a number of wise teachers, among them the famous Saint Finnian, who attracted many of the brightest intellects in Europe to the small town of Clonard where he taught. It was here that Columba acquired his great love of calligraphy and devoted much of his time to copying the rare manuscripts of the community. From the ages of twenty-five to forty, he travelled around Ireland teaching and setting up monasteries. He is credited with establishing thirty-seven, one of which was the renowned monastery of Kells where the Scriptures were transcribed into what is now known as the Book of Kells. It is believed that some of the chapters of that famous book were transcribed at the abbey in Iona.

That explains why, as an extended part of this pilgrimage to Iona, we later stood in a long queue at Trinity College in Dublin to see the Book of Kells. It was a hot day, my feet were aching and the people in front, moving forward in single file, seemed to be not advancing at all. Could it possibly be worth the pain? But when my turn finally came and I stood in front of the page from Saint Luke's Gospel that had been opened for that particular day I was utterly spellbound. The exquisite artistry of the illuminated capital letters, the perfection of each delicately rendered word was heart-stoppingly beautiful. I found myself in tears! I was never really prepared for the emotional impact of being in intimate touch with a distant past. In those few moments I was transported across 1400 years to the desk of some unknown monk who transcribed this page with such respect and love that no design could be too intricate, no detail too elegant and no skill too finely honed to express it. But more than that, I was suddenly stricken with an awareness of the casual and thoughtless way in which I handled these same Scriptures and the unthinking manner in which I took all books completely for granted. I stood there transfixed until the security guard touched me gently on the arm and indicated the long line of people waiting behind me, checking my embarrassed apology with the whispered assurance that it happened to everyone.

It's very likely that Columba would never have left Ireland if, saint that he was, he had not also possessed a healthy strain of human frailty. It is told that when one of the local princes violated the sanctuary of his church and killed a noble hostage, Columba avenged him by killing 3000 of his followers. It was not enough that they were pagans and that he attributed his victory to the power of Christianity. The elders of the Irish church promptly excommunicated him and he himself was plunged into deep remorse for what he had done. It was decided that his excommunication would be lifted if he left Ireland and gave his life to bringing the Good News of the Gospel of Christ to some pagan place. But there was one further stipulation: he was not to return to Ireland, and the place where he settled had to be out of sight of his beloved homeland. He and his companions headed to the islands off the coast of Northern Scotland. They landed on two of them but the dim outline of the Irish coast could still be seen in the distance. It was only when they stood on a hill on the island of Iona that their homeland was at last lost from sight. They named the place Carn-Cul-ri-Eirinn, the hill with its back to Ireland. Then they pulled ashore the fragile coracle that had brought them through the stormy Hebridean seas and began the work of founding a monastery and setting up a self-sufficient community.

It was the beginning of a long and fascinating history. Columba's saintliness, his scholarship and his charismatic leadership were such that flocks of pilgrims made their way to the island. The community expanded rapidly and more fields had to be cultivated to feed not only the monks but the increasing number of visitors. The first church and abbey were built and Iona became a holy place for all of Europe. Columba's missionaries went out from Iona to take the Gospel into all of Britain, beginning with Scotland, where more than a hundred churches were founded in his lifetime, and reaching even to the south of England. Columba died in 596, but the Celtic church he had founded expanded in numbers and grew in strength. It is significant that this same church became confident enough in time to split from Rome after certain differences of opinion, and it remained autonomous for many centuries.

For its fourteen centuries of often turbulent history, Iona has remained holy soil. It was at times invaded by Vikings and Norsemen, who left death and destruction in their wake. Sometimes the monks had to abandon the island to save the lives of their entire community. Many times its buildings were left in ruins, sometimes at the hands of brutal invaders, sometimes simply from neglect. Such was the case after the Protestant Reformation when the whole concept of monasteries became anathema and in 1561 the Scots Parliament, following the example of King Henry VIII of England, passed an act suppressing all monasteries. But in each century from the pre-Christian time of the Druids to this present day, Iona has survived as a holy place sanctified by its ancient and sacred past, by the blood of its martyrs and by the fervour and prayers of its pilgrims.

4 Monastic Life Again

It was at Iona that I had my first experience of seeing archaeologists at work. We came on them as we walked from the
pier to the abbey, a small group of people of all ages, patiently
sifting through the soil of the site marked off in the abbey
grounds. Old or young, they all had the same look of absorbed
concentration, utterly committed to their task, working in
silence, oblivious of passers by. I was to become intensely
aware in that week of what we owe to these skilful midwives
of history.

Certainly it was to them that we owed most of the
knowledge we acquired of Iona's past, that it was the place
where kings had been brought to be buried, sixty of them in
all — forty-eight Scottish, four Irish and eight Norwegian —
and that the last of these kings was buried there in the eleventh century before William the Conqueror invaded England.
Shakespeare claimed that Duncan and his murderer, Macbeth,
were among them. It was the archaeologists who revealed,
among so many other things, that the cobbled path they had
uncovered from Martyrs' Bay to the west door of the abbey was
the route of the funeral processions of the chiefs and kings,
and that the mound still visible at the landing site was where
the bier rested after being brought ashore.

It came as a moment of revelation to me that part of my
own history was connected to this place. The first convent of
the Sisters of Mercy in the Christchurch diocese had been
named St Colmekill's. (In Gaelic, Iona is called Chaluim-Chille,
translated as Colme-kill.) I thought of that pioneer band of
courageous young women, the first Sisters of Mercy who, in
1878, came to the West Coast of New Zealand's South Island

16

from Ennis in Ireland. They had travelled 20,000 kilometres by sailing ship across two oceans and I felt they were every bit as intrepid as Saint Columba and his followers in their frail coracle. Those women had also travelled to a place where they could no longer see their own country, not just across the water, but half a world away. I stood on the island of Colme-kill and thought of the convent of Colmekill in distant Hokitika.

There were as many surprises for me within the walls of the abbey as without. For one thing, I found myself living again the religious life I had been familiar with since the first day I had entered the convent. It was something of a shock, but it had all the quality of long familiarity. The abbey, which was in the care of the Church of Scotland, was the home of a religious community headed by a young Presbyterian minister and his wife. We were booked to stay in the abbey itself with about twenty other people who were there for the week's seminar. The rest of the course members were staying at a big youth hostel just up the road. The place was packed with young people, many camping outside, because it was still holiday time and the island of Iona has a great attraction for the young. When they all came down to the cathedral for the evening service each night they filled the big church to its limit.

I fell easily into the rhythm of a monastic routine. We followed a familiar daily timetable marked by the ringing of bells. There was a call bell that rang through the abbey to announce the beginning of each day, with the time for breakfast so strategically placed that if you didn't get up with the ringing of that bell, you were late for the first community meal of the day! The long tables in the refectory were arranged in the familiar inverted U form, with the heads of the community sitting at the top table. A book was read during the first part of each meal as we ate our food in silence. Two community members served on the tables and the dishes were handed down both sides of the U in the time-honoured way. There was no question of slipping unobtrusively into your place if you came late to a meal. Rather, you went to the middle of the floor and bowed to the 'superior' before taking your place at table, a custom I knew well.

We were entrusted with a certain part of the abbey to clean each day and a list of 'charges' was issued on the first day. Another 'novice' and I were given the task of looking after the library. Behind the door was a list of instructions: we were to mop the wooden floor on Monday and oil it on Tuesday, we were to dust certain bookshelves on one day and others on another, we were to open all windows to the same level, we were to wash the cleaning cloths on Friday . . . And, true to every convent timetable, there was simply not enough time to get it all done before the next bell rang.

As I followed the monastic order of each day at the abbey of Iona — morning prayer, meals, silence, study, work, evening prayer, night prayer — I was struck by the fascinating paradox of it all. This was the Church of Scotland whose Presbyterian tradition had rejected the whole idea of monastic life. And here, on Iona, it was rediscovering that life and living it with great respect and in its most traditional form. Ironically, the Catholic religious congregation to which I belonged, having clung faithfully to the monastic way of life over all the years, was now reassessing its value for those engaged in an active ministry, seeking new insights and experimenting with new forms. And not only my Order, but every other religious Order engaged in active work within the Catholic church. Instead of being securely enfolded each day within a strict timetable regulated by the ringing of bells, religious women and men were now being offered greater individual freedom and being invited to collaborate in finding creative ways of expressing the spirit of the religious life in the contemporary world. New wineskins for new wine!

5 *Pain and Paradox*

All this was, of course, part of the much greater paradox that is called history, and history has a habit of unfolding itself in its own benign and inexorable way. Four hundred years ago, when the Augustinian priest Martin Luther challenged the Church of Rome to reform itself, the church, grown complacent if not arrogant with the centuries, was in no mood to listen. Eventually the reformers and the church leaders hardened against each other to such an extent and became so implacably polarised that there was no alternative but to separate. What had begun as a timely protest and a legitimate call for reform became instead the Protestant Reformation, which broke the unity of the church, and many divergent branches were to spring to life from the ancient tree. As the Book of Wisdom says when speaking of death, 'it looked like annihilation'. And it has to be acknowledged that Christian history was less than benign in the centuries immediately following the Reformation. Wars were fought between nations espousing the opposing factions of Protestantism and Catholicism. Each side persecuted the other and the blood of martyrs cemented each in the certainty that truth was theirs.

All the protesting churches took their stand around the Bible and gave it a central place in their worship. This was done to the almost complete exclusion of the Eucharistic meal. Most of them built up an intense fear of the Mass, which they associated with popery and what they perceived as the worst excesses of Rome. The altar was removed from the central place it had held in every church over the centuries and was either discarded altogether or relegated to the sacristy or even to the porch to be used as a hat stand. In its place at centre stage in every sanctuary was placed the lectern holding the Bible, symbol of the heart of Protestantism. The Protestants now saw all the ancient symbols of devotion, such as statues and paintings and stained-glass windows, as a form of idolatry and they countered by building churches which, in their plain austerity, reflected their more severe and self-abnegating approach to religion. In those instances where they took over existing churches, they systematically removed all evidence of the Roman influence by destroying statues, stained-glass windows and religious paintings. Some of these may well have been no loss to posterity, but many were irreplaceable works of art.

The Catholic church, for its part, settled in for a long siege and its fortress mentality was to last for over 400 years. In this time all the growth and development of religious thought that comes naturally with the passage of time was so inhibited as to be virtually non-existent. Growth does not flourish in a climate of fear and suspicion and distrust of change. Instead the church took refuge in the rule of law and the movement of the Holy Spirit in the hearts of its members was gravely fettered. Instinctively, the church saw the Holy Spirit itself as scarcely to be trusted, as too unpredictable, too full of surprises, too ready altogether to inspire freedom and risk-taking and spontaneous response in the human heart. It was not politically correct in those years for Catholics to have devotion to the Holy Spirit and for the first part of my life, the Holy Spirit scarcely rated a mention in the prayer and devotion of the church. I knew virtually nothing of the special attributes of this third Person of the Blessed Trinity and it is no coincidence that when, in my middle life, I at last came on a book about the Holy Spirit, it was entitled *The Forgotten God*.

This form of Catholicism, engendered by the trauma of the Protestant Reformation, centred its worship firmly on the Eucharist to the almost complete exclusion of the Bible. The Bible was seen as a dangerous book from which the ignorant could make false interpretations and spawn further heresy. The clergy in their seminaries were now trained with much greater rigour to equip them to mediate the Word of God in Scripture to the laity, who were discouraged from reading the Bible in their own right. I can well remember smarting with indignation at the Protestant taunt that 'Catholics are not allowed to read the Bible', but the fact remains that almost my only contact with the Holy Book was when the priest read it to us at Mass each Sunday and then interpreted it in the sermon that followed. Even in the convent we read only the New Testament. We looked askance at Protestants confidently walking round with their Bibles under their arms, blissfully unaware that they were tottering on the brink of a spiritual abyss! Catholics in those days dealt in certainties. We possessed the whole truth. No doubts. No questioning. No danger.

For Catholics the Eucharist was all important, whether offered as a holy sacrifice to God in the Mass, or eaten as spiritual food in Holy Communion, or adored as a 'real presence' in the tabernacle of every altar. We attended Mass every Sunday under pain of serious sin, hoping that we did it also from motives of faith and love, with some degree of freedom and gladness in our hearts. We received the Body of Christ in the form of a small white host, which was an unleavened bread. We knelt at the altar rail and received the host reverently on our outstretched tongues, rooted in the teaching that only the priest could take the holy bread in his hand. For us, the 'real presence' meant that some of the hosts that had not been consumed in communion were 'reserved' in the tabernacles of our churches. This practice, introduced at a time when death came on people more immediately and with less warning, ensured that the sick and dying could receive Holy Communion at a moment's notice.

Whatever the original intent, the presence of Christ in the tabernacle effectively turned every Catholic church into a haven of prayer for any moment of any day. Who could forget the

21

atmosphere of the churches of that era? — the silence, the stillness, the light filtered through the deep reds, blues and greens of stained glass into a dim interior, the subtle fragrance of incense, beeswax candles and flowers, the statues and paintings and, most of all, the flickering red glow of the sanctuary lamp, which was the sign to us that Christ was present in the tabernacle.

But if the 'real presence' was the source of our greatest personal intimacy with God, we never had the slightest doubt that it was the Mass that was pre-eminent. 'It's the Mass that matters!' Those words were at the heart of all Catholicism for centuries, but it was Irish Catholics, in the face of unrelenting persecution, who made them singularly their own. I took that slogan into my heart from earliest childhood. Perhaps it was the alliteration that helped to commit the maxim to lasting memory. Perhaps it was the passion and conviction of the theology it encapsulated so succinctly. Most likely it was the history of ancestors who had risked their lives to celebrate the Mass in secret when it was forbidden under pain of death. Or it was the stories of young Irish priests, trained and ordained in France, being smuggled back into their own country to live as fugitives with a price on their heads. Or it was the mystic accounts of the Mass-stones consecrated as altars in secret hiding places in the hills and on which, when they were hunted down by the English, the blood of my forebears mingled with the blood of Christ. 'It's the Mass that matters!'

Was it any wonder, then, that for Catholics any change in this belief system, any new emphases, any fresh insights, any return to the spirit of the church in its first centuries, any growth to meet the needs of society in the present and the future, any healing of a fractured Christendom, in short any radical movement of the Holy Spirit within it, could be effected only by the most momentous event? And miraculously, blessedly, unexpectedly, such an event was to take place in my lifetime. It took the form of a Council of the Church. Councils of the Church, which bring together all the bishops in a solemn assembly, happen no more than once in a century and sometimes not as often as that. Pope John XXIII called such a council. His most shining hope was that it would help to heal the wounds that had split the Christian church into separated and mutually suspicious segments. But, before that could happen, he wanted the Catholic church to return to the openness and simplicity of the early church, in a form appropriate to the contemporary world yet unmistakably reflecting the spirit of its Founder. He wanted, he said, 'to restore the simple and pure lines which the face of Jesus' church wore at its birth'. The Second Vatican Council met in Rome on 11 October 1962.

My adult life spans rather neatly a significant period of time before the Second Vatican Council and a similar period after it: forty years before, and now over thirty years after. Like other Catholics of my age I have had the fascinating and often bewildering experience of inhabiting two vastly different religious worlds. We had the eerie experience of feeling the secure foundations on which, for a lifetime, we had built all our belief, our liturgy, our theology and our spirituality, rocking beneath us. And this state of affairs was effected, mark you, not by some reforming zealot, but by the College of Bishops in collaboration with the Pope himself. We had virtually no warning, but there it was: we were faced with entirely new emphases in scripture, theology and liturgy, some of them at variance with what we had been taught to believe was absolute and unchanging. In middle age, women and men of my generation were confronted with the prodigious challenge of either embracing the new order and venturing into strange new paths, or of rejecting it and staying with what we had always known. I was one of those who, along with the great majority of Catholics, embraced change gladly. It was as if, in our collective consciousness, we had been waiting for this moment of renewal and humility and openness in the church, not just for the space of our own short lifetimes, but for 400 years.

For those who could not accept such radical change, however, the Second Vatican Council introduced a time of great suffering. Catholics were given little or no space to resolve their doubts and questions and the welter of emotions that went with them. The official church, authoritarian still, had fallen back on the familiar and traditional methods of dealing with its members, even while requiring of them that they break with some of that tradition. It said, in effect, this is how it's going to be in the future. And it relied on the obedience of the faithful to accept and conform. But the faithful had had little or no preparation for such change and the most faithful of the faithful, those who had held all the teaching of the church as absolute, were now subject to the deepest spiritual confusion. They had always given the greatest loyalty to the Pope and the bishops and now it was these very people who were testing their loyalty in a way they could not have conceived possible.

6 The Challenge of Change

People could scarcely be expected immediately to perceive that the church was in the process of rolling back 400 years of history, that it was struggling to clear itself of much of the distortion and false emphasis that had sprung up from its reaction to the Protestant Reformation.

The Council, in its document on the Liturgy published in 1963, reiterated what had always been church teaching — namely that Christ was as truly present in other forms as in the Eucharist. With infinite care the document explained that it in no way detracted from God's presence in the Eucharist to proclaim that God is equally present in the Word of Scripture and in the people gathered for worship and in the ordained minister who presides. But no matter how thoughtfully it was explained, Catholics felt they were being dealt an entirely new body of teaching. And the reality was that it was often scarcely explained at all. Many priests, in the midst of their busy pastoral duties, had been caught comparatively unawares by what was happening in Rome. Certainly they were disconcerted by the speed of change.

Theologians, liturgists and Scripture scholars had for decades been calling for such things as the use of indigenous language in public worship, for Mass to be said facing the people, for the restoration of Scripture to its rightful place. And these were the people advising the bishops gathered in Rome. But all too often the person in the pew knew little more than that the Vatican Council had decreed these changes and this was how it had to be in future. People had little way of realising that these things had in fact been in the offing for many years, that they were not new at all, but rather a faithful return to the practices of the early centuries of Christianity, that, far from abandoning the traditions of the church, we were going back to them. But this was little comfort to those who now watched in unqualified dismay as, to accommodate the changes, the interiors of their churches were altered beyond recognition.

The church has always had a deep understanding of the extraordinary power of symbols in the forming and moulding of human consciousness. It had known, for instance, that little had to be put into words when the altar of every church provided a unique focal point at the centre of the sanctuary, drawing all attention to itself from the moment one entered the door. The absence of a Bible, on the other hand, was a symbol in itself. The Scriptures chosen to be read at Mass had been included with the prayers of the Mass in a book or missal placed on a small stand at the side of the altar. There was never any doubt then that, if the liturgy of the church were to undergo radical change, the old symbols would have to be changed. And changed they were. At one time or another in the next two decades, every Catholic greeted with either joy or horror the reorganisation of their parish church. Few of these changes were carried out without opposition, some of it passionate in the extreme, and, sadly, the real drama and history of the events that were unfolding were often lost in the accompanying brouhaha.

For Catholics, the action that carried the greatest historical significance was the restoration of the lectern to a central place in their worship. By doing this the church was, after four centuries, inviting its members to open their hearts and minds to embrace freely the Holy Book. That was history indeed and Martin Luther might well be permitted a smile in Heaven! In the renewal of the parish church where I worshipped when these changes were first implemented, a European model was followed: the lectern was placed at the end of the church facing the altar and at Mass when the Scriptures were being read it commanded all our attention, with every head turned towards it. Then, as the priest walked the length of the church to the altar, we turned to focus all our attention on the Eucharist. In my present parish the arrangement is different but the symbolism is the same. The altar and the lectern stand side by side, each beautifully formed from indigenous woods, the work of a local artist, each equal in status, neither more central than the other.

But the changes did not end with the establishment of equality between the altar and the lectern. The general upheaval might not have been so devastating for many Catholics if things had stopped there. The question that now arose was what was to be done with the tabernacle? This was the centre of devotion for so many Catholics because it contained 'the real presence'. The implication was that the only way to have an intimate encounter with the person of Jesus was by 'making a visit' which, in the Catholic idiom, meant going to a church and praying to him present in the tabernacle. It was not that this devotion did not provide the devout Catholic with an authentic spiritual experience. It most certainly did. But, like so much else, the emphasis had gone all wrong. Even the word 'real' in the term 'real presence' tended to exclude other authentic ways of experiencing the presence of Christ. And as for other Christians who did not have this 'real' presence, we preferred not to ponder their plight!

There is no doubt, however, that the church had always encouraged this devotion as a means of holiness for its members, and with the passage of time it had become more and more central. Once again it was the symbols that spoke: if the altar was at the centre of the sanctuary, the tabernacle was set at the centre of the altar. The tabernacle dominated the altar. The message was unmistakable. But now the message had to be unlearned and that required that the symbolism be changed. As the tabernacle was removed from the altar of each parish church and relocated to an inconspicuous position, it felt to many people as though the very heart of their religious devotion was being torn out; in some bewildering way it was an insult to the Lord they loved. It was not much use to explain that, for many centuries, the church had never kept the sacred host reserved, that there had been no such thing as a tabernacle in a church, that the custom had been introduced primarily to provide Holy Communion for the sick and dying in plague-ridden times. Devotion to the 'real presence' had sprung up spontaneously. It was a beautiful devotion and should remain so, but its place belonged not in the public worship associated with the altar but in the realm of private prayer.

And it was here that much of the problem lay. Private and public prayer had become so deeply entangled in our spiritual lives that we had little understanding of either. The philosophy of the Renaissance, which had its religious counterpart in the Reformation, had been passionately individualistic. And the Roman church, for all its distaste for the Reformation, was nevertheless affected by the thinking that motivated it. Even the Mass, that most significant form of public worship, gradually became more and more a place for individual piety. People went to Mass to pray their personal prayers rather than to unite with one another in a great communal act of worship. And the seating in every church was entirely suited to their purpose. The straight rows of seats meant you did not have to be aware of other people. You could be as alone and withdrawn from others as you pleased — an individual at prayer.

Theologically the church taught that the Mass was the con-summate prayer of the Christian community. But in those forty years of my life before the Second Vatican Council, although I knew the teaching, I had virtually no experience of the reality. The symbols told me otherwise. They spoke of one hundred individuals gathered at this parish Mass, rather than just the one community. So when all else was renewed in our churches — the altar, the lectern, the chair for the presiding priest, the tabernacle — it still needed a suitable arrangement of the seats to imbue us with the truth that Christ was also present in the people gathered. The usual form that this takes is a great half-circle around altar and lectern, with seats arranged so that people can see one another and know that each is a sister or brother in this Christian community. Many churches may not have renewed themselves to this degree, but most will give some evidence that the work has begun. This is all very fine now, thirty years later. At the time, it looked to some as though 'they' were tearing out the seats, creating an atmosphere where it was impossible to say one's prayers, jumping on the 'caring and sharing' bandwagon of the 1960s, destroying the silence, dismantling a precious spiritual environment.

For many it was nothing short of heartbreak to contemplate all this change. Some grieved in silence. Some felt so betrayed that they left the church. And some of stronger mettle set their faces against such 'desecration' and mobilised their followers to fight the agents of change with every modern weapon at hand, including the media. For a church that had always pre-sented a united front to the outside world and was skilled at keeping every sign of internal discord carefully hidden, this was new ground indeed. Parish priests and bishops alike were suddenly being held accountable to their outraged flocks and, far from excommunicating their dissident members, were re-luctantly forced to confront them, not behind closed doors but in the public arena. I remember the late Bishop Ashby telling me with wry humour, though admittedly retrospective, of how he felt when he arrived for work early one morning to find the television cameras set up on the steps of the cathedral and an interview with a disenchanted member of his diocese already in progress. And it was the most conservative, if not reaction-ary, members of the church who were acting in this disorderly and entirely radical way!

It was hardly what Pope John had in mind when he called a council so that the windows of the church could be opened to let in some fresh air. This was no gentle breeze, this was a gale. The fortress was being blown apart.

In the midst of all this internal turmoil of our own, it was little wonder that we were relatively unaware of what was happening in other churches. I remember the delight I experienced when talking to a Protestant friend to discover that, just as we were restoring the Bible to our worship, so they were restoring the Eucharist. The altar was being brought back into a prominent place in their churches and the Eucharist was being celebrated with much greater regularity. And not without conflict, either! The remnants of the Reformation were still clinging to the religious consciousness of many Protestants. Some of them had to be sure that the restoration of the altar was not part of a popish plot to lure them back to Rome. People in the local Protestant churches were in need of the same sensitive re-education as their Catholic counterparts down the street. Fears had to be allayed as old truths were rehabilitated. There was a balance to be adjusted, and emphases that had been thrown out of kilter by the Reformation had to be set right. The altar was not in competition with the lectern; it was part of the same sacred whole. And, just as Catholics of that era held their newly acquired Bibles in their hands with a reverence that bordered on awe, and were filled with excitement as they began tentatively to discuss the Scriptures together for the first time, so Protestants made their first approaches to the Eucharist with a like reverence and perhaps even greater awe, learning to become familiar with a beautiful food that they had eaten comparatively rarely in the past. It was as if the Catholic and Protestant churches had locked themselves away for four centuries clutching their respective treasure to themselves, polishing, cherishing and refining it until the other was ready to receive it.

And for many there was unqualified pleasure in any coming together of the two former antagonists. I shall always remember the early-morning prayer sessions in which I took part when our community first went to live in Aranui. Once a week, at 6.30 in the morning, we came together: the local Salvation

Army officer, the leader of an evangelical church, the Presbyterian and Anglican ministers and some of the laity of their churches and we three nuns. There was no doubt that, as we reflected on a particular Scripture passage, we sometimes became acutely aware of our differing theologies, but when we turned to prayer we were completely at one, as we were at the breakfast we shared afterwards and as we increasingly became in our respective activities in the wider community. And it was somewhere about that time, too, that I was invited to Timaru to speak to a South Island assembly of Presbyterian women. It concluded with a celebration of the Eucharist by a woman priest in an atmosphere of such homage and reverence that I found myself shaken by emotion to be part of it. It only remained for me to go to a funeral in a Presbyterian church in Ashburton, and find myself gazing up at beautiful stained-glass windows, to get the distinct impression that the wounds inflicted by the Reformation were being healed.

During that week at Iona back in 1979 I found all these things being processed in my mind. On the Thursday of our week there, when we were sitting in the refectory eating our evening meal in silence, the head of the abbey community came to me with a whispered request. He told me that the news had just come through that Earl Mountbatten had been assassinated by the IRA in Northern Ireland. I had been one of those preparing the night prayer so would I mind saying a prayer for all concerned in this tragic event? So that night there I was, New Zealand Irish, Catholic to the core, kneeling in an abbey under the auspices of the Presbyterian church, praying for an Anglican English aristocrat killed by the Catholic side of what was perceived as a sectarian war. I prepared that prayer with more than usual care.

We left Iona on the Friday. We had received much intellectual stimulus from the seminar, but most of all we had experienced hospitality, friendship, prayer and peace. And we had

31

been immersed in the mystical history of a holy and ancient island that had been plundered and ravaged by hostile invaders and whose Christian inhabitants had suffered persecution, bloodshed and martyrdom. But for fourteen centuries it had survived. The descendants of Saint Columba had died out and risen up again many times over that long history.

Before we left Iona I went to read once again the poem carved on a marble column in the cloister:

> I saw a stranger yestreen
> I put food in the eating place
> Drink in the drinking place
> Music in the listening place
> And in the sacred name of the Triune
> He blessed myself and my house
> My cattle and my dear ones
> And the lark sang —
> 'Often, often, often
> Comes the Christ in the stranger's guise'

The poet was Columba and it was written in the sixth century, but the song belongs in every Christian heart of any age.

7 Ireland

I never really wanted to go to Ulster. We'd come to Ireland to study certain community projects. We didn't have any reason for going to the North, now did we? Sister Helen (known to her family as Betty) lived in my community at home in Aotearoa New Zealand. She had close family connections in Lurgan, a town about 30 kilometres from Belfast. Her mother had come from there. But she had said she'd be happy if I rang them while I was in Ireland and gave them her love and greetings. She did not expect me to go to Northern Ireland to see them. And certainly no one in Southern Ireland expected us to be venturing into what was, in 1979, a dangerous war zone.

The impression I got in the South was that the six counties of the North didn't exist anyway. In that year there were bombings and murders and military attacks that suggested something very near to a full-scale war. But in the Republic, not so many kilometres away, no one spoke of it. It was a strange silence. I wondered if the Irish of the South, having acquired their own independence and the recognition of their place among the nations of the world, might even be a little ashamed of their Catholic cousins who were still fighting the English and going about it in a distinctly violent and messy way.

In the end I decided that the real reason for their silence was simply that they could not bear to talk about it. I felt that every single person in Ireland was carrying a secret burden of sorrow that no outsider could ever hope to understand. After long centuries of resistance, here they were themselves, a generation on from the humiliation of foreign rule, with their independence attained. They were living under their own sophisticated parliamentary system that owed nothing to their former rulers, their confidence in themselves growing with each succeeding year and Europe waiting with open arms to embrace them. But it was all so much dust in their mouths as long as they were denied the unity of their country. Their own national wound, which should have been well into the process of healing, was being kept open and bleeding by what was still going on in the North.

In a strange kind of way it seemed to me that while *I* could afford to indulge myself in the luxury of anger, *they* could not. I wanted to *talk* about what was going on. I wanted to hear their version of earlier events and how the partition had come to be. Naively, I had thought that in Ireland of all places this would be possible. Even if those events were just outside their own memory, their parents and grandparents must have known what it felt like for their country to become a pawn in English party politics. Surely they had told their children about it. It quite escaped me at the time that there was a generation of people in my own country who knew virtually nothing about the terrible things that happened in the Pacific War. And yet many of their fathers had fought in the jungles and been prisoners of war in the Japanese camps. And there were many people who had little first-hand knowledge of the Depression of the 1930s even though both their parents might have lived through it. We simply don't talk about that part of ourselves where the memory is still hurting.

But at the time, fresh from teaching School Certificate history in distant New Zealand, I felt that my antipodean students could have told these people all about the history of their recent past. And they'd learnt it from English-sourced history books, for goodness' sake. They knew, for instance, that only the House of Lords had stood between Ireland and the right to its own parliament in 1893 and again in 1912, and that they'd done it by overriding the elected representatives of the people in the House of Commons. They could have told why the British Parliament in 1914 didn't implement a Home Rule Act that had been passed in its own parliament two years before. And as for the Easter Rising of 1916, they could have submitted five neatly tabulated reasons telling why it failed and five more telling why it succeeded. And any School Certificate class worth its salt could have written an essay on the subject of the partition of Ireland. So what was wrong with these people? Arrogance, especially in oneself, is not a pretty sight when viewed retrospectively.

For all that, we had a wonderful time in Ireland. The country was as beautiful as I thought it should be. The hospitality was as warm and spontaneous and open-handed as I had imagined. But the flow of humour and the sheer humanity of the people was far beyond anything I had anticipated. It was enough. There seemed no point at all in any talk of going to Northern Ireland.

But I had counted without Donald Malloch. There is no idealism quite so deep and pure and so unyielding and irrational as the idealism of the Scottish Celt! He had already made up his mind that he was going to Northern Ireland and, more than that, that I was going with him. We were a Presbyterian minister and a Catholic nun and we were going to go there and give witness to the fact that things could be different.

I have to admit that the response to my phone call when I finally made it left me feeling more than a little disconcerted. I was completely unprepared for the level of excitement it seemed to generate. It was not a very clear telephone line. I was Betty? The voice was high with incredulity. No, I wasn't Betty, but I was a member of her community. I was in Ireland? I lived with Betty and I was in Ireland? The voice rose half an octave with each question. When could they expect me? Well, as a matter of fact, I didn't think I'd be able to get up to Lurgan this time. (I actually said, 'this time'!) I don't think it was heard. If it was, it was brushed aside, irrelevant. What was this? I had come all the way from New Zealand. I lived with their cousin Betty! And I was saying that I couldn't come to see them! But

I *had* to come to see them. Mammy would be heartbroken if I didn't come. They would all be heartbroken. I was to come and *stay*! Oh no, I couldn't do that. I was not travelling alone. And how, in Heaven's name, could that make any difference? the voice wanted to know. Any number were welcome, and who was there who could doubt that? And then a certain thought seemed to cast a ray of light on her bewilderment. 'Ah,' she said reassuringly, 'you'll be perfectly safe, you know. We'll see to it that nothing happens to you!' I was ashamed.

We were to be in Lurgan for lunch. We drove through the lovely countryside on a golden, autumn morning. It seemed entirely unreal to think that just a few kilometres further on, in that part of the country towards which we were heading, people were actually killing one another. But the moment we crossed the border, the unreal became the real. There, lined up neatly at the side of the road as though in a parking lot, ready for an immediate take-off, were the huge armoured tanks from the British army, the long fingers of their guns pointing straight towards us. It was a chilling sight. Nothing could have brought home to us more explicitly that we had entered a war zone. The tanks were painted in the standard camouflage colours of brown and green, but in contrast to the bright sunlight they looked black and sinister and uncompromisingly hostile and threatening.

We negotiated the intricacies of the streets of Lurgan and, following the instructions that Mona, our hostess, had given us on the phone, we turned at last into the narrowest little street I'd ever seen, and entered what could only be described as an enclave. The backyards of some fifteen houses opened out on to this little lane, clustering around it protectively and closing it in completely except for the entrance through which we had come. We were, in all truth, in a Catholic ghetto. There were people everywhere. The sunshine had brought everyone out to their back steps and children were playing in the narrow street as of right. It's just possible, of course, that the neighbours knew that visitors from New Zealand were due to arrive and we drove slowly through a sea of faces, every one of them smiling. When we stopped at Mona's gate, there were shouts of 'They've arrived!', doors flew open, people came running towards us with arms outstretched and for the first time we heard the singular Northern Irish accent and it was uttering just the one word, 'Welcome, welcome, welcome!'

I've never known an experience to match that one — it was like being enfolded in a warm, chaotic and wildly happy blanket. The family had all gathered from far and wide, with more to come that afternoon. Glory be to God, will you listen to their lovely accents! And she lives with our cousin, Betty, would you believe it? No, no, not Australia, New Zealand! And tell me, have they travelled all the way from Dublin today? Sure, what's Dublin to them? They've come from the other end of the earth! And only for a day? Oh, the pity of it!

But in the midst of all this happy clamour there were moments of sudden shyness, small, barely perceptible silences, an involuntary body language that spoke of uncertainty as they were introduced to Donald. He wasn't just a Protestant, glory be to God, he was a Protestant minister! I wouldn't have been surprised if they'd blessed themselves. But if he noticed any of this momentary awe, Donald Malloch gave no sign. He took each person's hand in both of his and, with tears very near the surface, he exuded from his kindly face all the concern of his heart. It occurred to me that he was giving witness on behalf of every Presbyterian minister in Northern Ireland.

Later, it was Mona who had the inspiration. She said suddenly, 'Donald, would you come with me and we'll go and find the Presbyterian minister. We'll tell him we have a New Zealand colleague of his visiting us and we'll ask him to dinner.' She held out her hand to Donald. Would he go with her, I ask you? They were out the door and on their way before you could say, 'Battle of the Boyne'! But it was now Donald's turn to register shock. Not only did Mona not know who the Presbyterian minister was, she had no idea where the church would be and she was totally unfamiliar with the part of town where it was situated. It was not a big town; she had simply never been to that particular part. Later, when Helen visited Lurgan and stayed for three months, she was to tell us that she never became used to shopping in the Catholic half of the main street and never setting foot in a Protestant shop in the other half. When you came to the last Catholic shop, you turned round and came back. Similarly, the Protestants from the other end never crossed that invisible line on the street, which had all the characteristics of a hostile border to a foreign country.

The Reverend Jim Matthews, God bless him, happened to be in his church when they finally found it. He'd had no warning when he began that day that such a thing could happen, but he did not hesitate for a moment. In fact, he leapt at the invitation. He told Donald later that he could never have gone into those particular streets under any other circumstances because he would have been at risk from both sides of that awful sectarian conflict. Now he was going by invitation and he asked Mona if his wife could come as well. He directed them to the house and, as Donald told me later, he was inside for only a few seconds before his wife came running down the front path, taking off her apron as she ran. It seemed as though the words of Scripture were bursting into silent song in their hearts: 'Blessed are the feet of those who bear good tidings'.

I have no capacity to convey in words what happened after that. From the moment that Jim and Jean Matthews came into that house the atmosphere was electric — not with hostility, but with joy. Six of us sat down at the table and Mona's tiny kitchen became a banqueting hall. Everyone else gathered round us, listening to our conversation, waiting on us. But it was when we adjourned to the lounge that it all began to really happen. I won't say that the New Zealand visitors were forgotten, but they came close to it. Everyone wanted to talk to the

Reverend Matthews or to his wife. Neighbours came in. I could hear scraps of conversation floating across the room. 'Ah Reverend, we were very sorry at what our boys did to the butcher's shop a couple of weeks ago.' 'And I was ashamed that some of our lads wrote what they did on the church hall.' They went back over this fight, that fire, the other break-in. It was not the big stuff of the conflict, but it was the run-of-the-mill, everyday bitterness that constantly fed its fires. I could hear apologies being made, words of sorrow pouring out, regret, pity for the extremes they'd come to, and both sides saying that it didn't have to be.

And the lasting picture I have is of an old woman looking up into Jim Matthews' face, his hand in both of hers, tears running down her cheeks as they silently shook their heads over the futility of it all.

At the height of all this, Mona announced that she was going to ring the convent to ask Sister Teresa to come. This was a much more significant decision than I would have expected. It became clear that, although all the girls in the family had gone to the Sisters of Mercy for their schooling, a nun had never been inside any of their homes. But they all thought the world of Sister Teresa; she had a great way with the youth. Still, I detected a small anxiety. Mona felt the need to tell us how busy Sister was and I could see she was preparing us in case she didn't come. I knew the 'busy nun' syndrome all too well and I found myself willing Sister Teresa to put aside whatever she was doing that afternoon and come to that house. This was an opportunity not likely to come her way again.

When she finally arrived, there was no mistaking the impact of her presence. Here was the equivalent of royalty if ever I saw it, such was the respect that they tendered her. One of the nuns from the convent was actually coming into their home. I was inclined to take a rather dim view of this circumstance, which seemed to display the distance that the nuns kept from the people. But I was on my own. The vibes coming from everyone else spoke of nothing but excitement and delight.

She was brought across the room to be presented to the Reverend Matthews. The meeting between the minister and the nun had a touch of drama about it that was not lost on their audience. We watched them in silence. Sister Teresa, in her early thirties maybe, was a lovely woman, attractive in the new habit. She had a warm, easy manner and she came forward with a smile of such singular pleasure that it gave a kind of radiance to her face. The minister received her with a formality that had not been present in the other meetings. He told her that he had heard of her on former occasions and the good work that she was doing in Lurgan. He congratulated and thanked her. The Catholic sector swelled visibly with pride and pleasure that one of 'them' should be making such a generous acknowledgment of one of 'us'. Donald Malloch was well pleased with his colleague. His face was one huge, happy smile. As for me, I was fast becoming an emotional mess — and it was getting late. We'd been told we should get back across the border before nightfall.

At around the time that we should have been saying our goodbyes, the Reverend Matthews carried the Reverend Malloch off to show him his church and manse and no doubt to talk of things Presbyterian. I remained behind in the gathering dusk to be shown the family photo albums. It was then that the harsh reality of their lives came home to me with an almost unendurable impact.

I couldn't take it in at first, but gradually it dawned on me that in nearly every photo, be it of a wedding, a birthday celebration or some other family occasion, there were young men who had been killed. As a page was turned and I waited to be told who was in the group, a silence would fall. Then someone would say something like, 'Poor Jimmy' or 'It's been four years, God help us' or 'His mother has never been the same'. In the end, pointing to a handsome, laughing best man or to a boy who should have been in the sixth form, I said, 'Are you saying that this young man is dead?' And they'd tell me. He was shot in cold blood in his own car. Or he was taken out behind a barn in the country and executed. Or he was 'active' in the 'movement' and was killed in an ambush. Or he was in Longkesh jail with a life sentence. I was completely dumbfounded. They seemed almost casual about it. They even had little arguments about times and places. It was June of '74. No, it was August. No, it was June, I remember because it was just after Marie's wedding. I thought it was in '73. No, no . . . Then, in an instant, we'd be saying how beautiful the bride looked.

It was all too much for me. The euphoria of the afternoon was fast dissipating into black despondency. I was cold with the proximity of horror, shocked and upset. And I was angry with Donald Malloch. He knew very well that we should be leaving before dark and now I sensed that we were going to have a struggle to leave at all. By the time my travelling companion returned, ecumenical relations had reached their lowest ebb. And, just as it was looking as though we were on our way at last, it transpired that a promise had been made to Sister Teresa that we would call at the convent before we left. It was the last straw. I immediately protested, but it was too late.

Night was falling as we drove in silence through the large iron gates and up the drive to the convent. The dark bulk of the building stood out against the skyline, its dimensions out of all proportion to the size of the town. Sister Teresa threw open the door, waiting to do the honours. She gave three long rings on the door bell to indicate that visitors had arrived. I could only marvel that we did exactly the same thing in every convent I'd ever been in on the other side of the world. It was a signal for everyone to put down whatever she was doing and come immediately to welcome them. Now, in an instant, nuns appeared from all sides. I was presented to each one as Sister Pauline, a Mercy nun from faraway New Zealand. One after the other they enfolded me in an all-encompassing embrace, kissed me on both cheeks and told me how welcome I was. An *Irish* Mercy? they wanted to know. This had to be established. There were other Sisters of Mercy in the world, founded in places like France or Spain. Was I a daughter of Catherine McAuley? I was? Glory be to God!

In the midst of all this, I could hear the commotion that was going on behind me. The Reverend Mr Malloch, a Presbyterian minister from New Zealand, was being introduced to each of the nuns in turn. The Irish have a wonderful, innate and quite inimitable piece of choreography. Given the right kind of happy provocation, they let out a not unmusical scream, throw their arms high in the air, raise their eyes to heaven and, simultaneously and with great fervour, intone the words, 'Glory be to God', to which they sometimes add, 'and all his holy angels and saints'. If it is repeated at least thirty times, as it was in this instance, it takes on the quality of a musical mantra, which is essentially a prayer. Most of them were meeting their first Protestant!

In other circumstances I would have savoured every moment of all this, but by now I was obsessed with the desire to get on the road. There was no logic to support my preoccupation, since night had long since fallen. I should not have been surprised that, just when I thought it was appropriate to take our leave, my companion announced that he would like to go to the chapel to pray! Everyone else was delighted; his stock soared. We were escorted down endless corridors past statues of all the patron saints of Ireland: little blue lights flickered before those of Our Lady, red ones for Saint Patrick, flowers for Catherine McAuley. We knelt in what was undoubtedly a beautiful chapel and no one could have guessed that the ecumenical movement was in disarray. I knew that Donald was praying for peace and reconciliation for Northern Ireland and I was glad of it because I could get no further than an impassioned plea to God to get us safely home.

As we drove through the night, two things became evident: one was that we were the only car on the road and the other was that the roads were unusually dark. I have no doubt that this impression was heightened by my imagination, which was slightly out of control. But those roads did seem to lack the openness of those in New Zealand and in a country where the ambush was used extensively and sometimes mistakenly, it added to the feeling of menacing danger. But all seemed to be going safely by the time we reached the small town of Banbridge, so we were both completely dismayed to see two large shadowy figures in the middle of the road swinging torches back and forth to flag us down. They identified themselves as the police. Was the name Malloch, they wanted to know? Had we been visiting the town of Lurgan that day? Looking back, I can't help feeling that they knew how fear-inspiring they were, standing there in what we could now see were bulletproof jackets. They took their time, letting us sweat a little.

When they told us why they had stopped us, we could scarcely believe our ears. They'd had a ring from Mona. It appeared, they said, that we'd left a tape-recorder behind. Our friends had asked that we wait outside the Banbridge police station. They were on their way to bring it to us! I had already realised that I'd left the tape-recorder behind. I'd hoped to get some messages on tape to take home to Helen but, in the happy bedlam of that afternoon, this had proved impossible. I'd just said to Donald that I'd write and ask Mona to keep the tape-recorder and perhaps make a tape when the moment was right. But we counted without the generosity, the high spirits, the spontaneity, the immediacy of the family in Lurgan.

After twenty minutes they arrived with more people packed into a little Volkswagen than I had thought possible. It was late at night, but for them it was like the middle of the day. I remember hearing an Irishman say that if they can help it, the Irish never go to bed the same day as they get up! They tumbled out onto the silent street in high spirits, laughing and rejoicing that we were unexpectedly meeting again so soon. There were greetings and kisses all over again and they wanted to hear a full account of how we'd got on at the convent. Infected by their freedom of spirit and genuine interest, I leant against their little car and was ready to talk until midnight!

Donald and I arrived in Dublin very late that night, no doubt tired but happy. In truth, though, we were far too tired to know for sure if we were happy or not!

8 The Myth of the 'Other'

In retrospect, we were actually very happy. But we were also very perplexed. We had been given what seemed to us convincing evidence that people on both sides of that tragic civil war were hungering for peace; they wanted to be reconciled with one another. We could not believe that, by some extraordinary coincidence, we had stumbled on the one Catholic family and the one Protestant couple in all of Northern Ireland who wanted to say they were sorry to each other. There had been nothing superficial or hypocritical about that meeting; even the most hardened sceptic would have had to admit to its sincerity. We felt humbled and confounded that we had been the unwitting facilitators of this particular coming together and we knew in our bones that what we had experienced could have been replicated thousands of times given a similar set of circumstances. We decided that, if a large team of neutral facilitators representing both Catholics and Protestants could have been introduced into that riven society, the process of reconciliation could have begun. This may well be seen as an overly shallow solution to a deep-seated problem but, as solutions go, it at least has the merit of lateral thinking. And that's the most lasting impression I brought away from that experience — the need to think outside the entrenched positions and prejudices of history.

One of the saddest aspects of situations such as that in Northern Ireland is that both sides of the conflict claim the heritage of Christianity. And both sides share the same history in which the teaching of Christ was first betrayed. It goes back to the fourth century. When the young Christian church was taken under the wing of the Emperor Constantine, the idea of converting others by force was tragically begotten. It was tragic first because it had no foundation whatever in the teachings of Jesus and again, because of the suffering and horror it has engendered through the centuries. But the combination of strongly held belief with the possession of great power has always proved dangerous to the human psyche.

The young Christian church, which had endured constant persecution in its early centuries, now suddenly found itself with the military power of the Roman Empire at its disposal, and its leaders obviously found the temptation irresistible. It must have appeared to them much smarter, much more efficient and certainly much quicker to convert the pagan world to Christianity by the use of force. By comparison, the way that Jesus had prescribed appeared intolerably slow: the living of a life so transparently good that all people would be drawn to it. His way meant living a life of tolerance and forgiveness and love for all, as of a sister and brother. When we see how readily the human spirit is seduced by the prospect of having power over others, even when we use that power for what we believe is their good, we begin to perceive why Jesus went to such lengths to be utterly powerless. Although he had all power in heaven and earth at his disposal, he was bent on giving us a way that relied only on the power of love.

By the sixteenth century, when the Protestant Reformation split Christendom in two, all the precedents for the use of force were firmly in place. Crusaders had gone off with the full blessing of the church to drive the Muslims from the Holy Land. The Battle of Lepanto in 1571, which saw Christians triumph over Muslims, was even given a special feast day in the church calendar. In my own schooldays, I can remember thrilling with uncritical triumphalism to the majestic stanzas of the poem 'Lepanto', written this century by G. K. Chesterton in honour of that battle. Don John of Austria led the Christians to victory at that battle and crushed the infidel. I loved that poem:

In that enormous silence, tiny and unafraid
Comes up along a winding road the noise of the Crusade,
Strong gongs groaning as the guns boom far,
Don John of Austria is going to the war . . .

With such a tradition, it was seen as only natural that both Catholics and Protestants should take up arms and try to gain ascendancy over the other by force. The history of the wars and massacres and religious persecution of both sides make hard reading today. And some of that bloody conflict was fought with bitter and lasting results on Irish soil, culminating in triumph for the Protestants at the Battle of the Boyne in 1690.

The Protestant ascendancy placed the Catholic population in Ireland under crippling penal laws intended to bring them to heel. Those laws brought religious persecution to the Catholics; they also brought the loss of political power and economic ruin. In the 1840s the Irish suffered one of the worst famines in history, a famine made all the more devastating because it could have been alleviated. It's a bitter story. The Irish peasants had long been forced to live solely on potatoes while all the other food they produced, especially their corn, was sent to England. There the Tory party, backed by the landlords, kept a high tax on imported corn to prevent it coming in from foreign countries and thus lowering the price of bread. This policy of economic protection, by keeping the price of bread high, brought suffering enough to the poor of England, but it brought unqualified disaster to the Irish. In the wet summers of 1845 to 1847 corn was in short supply and England needed all she could get from her Irish province. But in Ireland, as all their corn was forcibly shipped to England, the potato crop rotted in the ground and they had no food. As the great Tory leader, Robert Peel, cried out in the House of Commons, 'Good God, are you to sit in Cabinet and calculate how much diarrhoea and bloody flux and dysentery a people can bear before it becomes necessary for you to provide them with food?'

In making such statements, Peel destroyed his own political career since the Tories saw him as a traitor. But he was too late. By 1848, when he at last got the hated Corn Laws repealed and wheat was allowed into England from Europe, a million Irish had died of starvation and a million more had emigrated.

One of the most subtle aspects of English rule was that the English harboured a deeply rooted contempt for the indigenous people of Ireland. It could be argued that the English in 1840 in Aotearoa New Zealand were treating the indigenous people at Waitangi with far greater respect than they had ever showed the Irish up to that time and for many decades afterwards. As far back as the Norman invasion, English writing confirms that they saw the Irish as an inferior race. And, in later times, they could see little hope for a people who laboured under the twin disadvantages of being both Irish and Catholic. This attitude was faithfully transmitted to the countries of the New World where the English planted their flag and assumed power, countries to which the Irish flocked, most often as semi-literate labourers. It is an attitude that lasted in our own country rather longer than we might care to admit, although I cannot claim to have been inhibited by it.

But even without the inherent racism in the English attitude towards the Irish, the Protestants in Ireland have a deep residue of fear towards Catholicism. A recent commission reaffirmed this, reporting 'widespread and deep fear and mistrust' among Northern Protestants about the Catholic church. Catholics are always bewildered by this. Not even their finely honed Celtic imaginations seem able to perceive how the other sees it. Irish Protestants carry in their hearts all the traditional fears of a minority under any system, especially one in which they see themselves as ruled by a Catholic majority. They have always perceived Catholicism as much more than a religion. They see it as a threatening political system with international dimensions. The slogan of the Orangemen that Home Rule would mean Rome Rule was the truth as they saw it. And until recent times, the Catholic church has done little to allay those fears. It is surely not difficult to see, for instance, how any Protestant would feel about the requirement, never rescinded but now in abeyance, that children of mixed marriages be brought up Catholic, or to understand their fear of Catholic control of education or of Catholic doctrine being imposed by the power of the state. These things have either gone or are fast disappearing in modern Ireland, but the attitudes and fears they engendered are not dissipated so easily.

An irrational fear of another person is always a destructive human emotion. When it comes to dominate the emotions of an entire group in its relationship to another group, it becomes a terrifying entity. Ultimately, each group has to find its own healing through the grace-filled change of heart of its individual members. It was something of this which we witnessed that day in Lurgan and which is evident all over Ireland. It remains for the leaders in government to work honourably for the solution that has begun and for which the people are yearning. For the Irish on both sides, and for the English, who have with appalling cynicism so often exploited Irish divisions for their own ends, this cannot come soon enough. If it does not, if fear continues to be drip-fed into the hearts of the people, it could finally take on the most neurotic, hysterical and malevolent face of all — the face of the racial, ethnic or religious myth.

We have no need to look back to our history books to see the workings of racial myth. We have all seen its horrendous effects. Powerful beyond belief, it sweeps ordinary people along with it and it can thrust a civilised, cultured and intelligent people towards the most hideous acts of barbarity. We can scarcely claim to be more civilised, more cultured or more intelligent than the German people of the 1930s. But, before we condemn them out of hand, we need to know beyond a shadow of doubt that we are not looking at the hidden reflection of our own face in that mirror.

Night after night on our television news we see the atrocities that are being committed in Bosnia (and if not there, then in some other part of the world). We see the grief, the sorrow, the humiliation, the despair of people separated from their loved ones, themselves on the run from murder and rape and other forms of unspeakable violence. We sit there watching them, knowing that we have not the slightest idea what it is all about, grappling with the futility of our own outrage.

But it is one thing to experience the depth of our own powerlessness in the face of such human suffering; it is quite another to realise that the most 'powerful' countries in the world seem to be as powerless as any one of us to effect a peaceful solution. In the end, it seems to me, we are left with just one constructive option. We can ponder how all this might have come about and ask where it began. And then we can make a prayerful and penetrating examination of our own lives to perceive if the seeds of such human conflict and division are already sown deep in our own hidden consciousness. Because those hatreds must have started somewhere. Somehow the myth that others are different must have been nourished year after year, inbred in one generation after the other until, at last, the people who are the objects of our contempt are made less human than we are. Ordinary people can become so deeply entrenched in this belief as to wipe from our consciousness the truth that the difference between us and them is very small indeed. And that is true of every other human being, regardless of colour, race, religion or ethnic origin. If I can be persuaded to believe otherwise, then I am well on the way to making Aotearoa New Zealand into a potential Northern Ireland, a Gaza Strip, or even a Bosnia or a Rwanda.

9 The Other's Shoes

As a first step, I might be well advised to check out the state of health of my imagination. This exercise can sometimes prove more than a little disconcerting, because if there is one human attribute that has suffered gravely from lack of development in our society, it must be the imagination. The imagination doesn't just get a bad press, it gets no press at all! It is seldom held up to the young as a gift to be aspired to and acquired by serious practice. When we want to affirm the young, we generally remark on their intelligence, their application, their co-ordination or their creative gifts. But if we ever say, 'She has a great imagination', we generally do so with our eyes raised towards heaven as if asking for help. We seldom rejoice at the early signs of a good imagination, so it's no wonder that most people grow up with very little sense of what a priceless gift it really is.

It is only by using imagination that we can place ourselves in another's shoes in any authentic way. We need to place ourselves inside the mind of the other, practise seeing how things look through their eyes, hear the nuances of words with their ears and feel with their emotions. Such an effort of the imagination enables us to take the mental leap across any dividing chasm to the place where the other is standing. It makes cross-identification possible. And when we can do that, we have acquired one of the most important human attributes, the one that is known as empathy, that solid, lasting, respectful and equalising basis of all true reconciliation.

Empathy, like every other good in our lives, has to be developed with practice. Left on its own, the imagination can sicken and turn in on itself, producing the worst expressions of narcissism. It is only when it becomes outward-looking that it fulfils its wonderfully healthful purpose in our lives. We first learn how to empathise by having other people empathise with us, just as we learn how to love through the experience of being loved. Some people go through much of their lives without either empathy or love and it is the saddest of all human deprivations.

Psychotherapists tell us that people come to them preoccupied with their own fear and despair, immersed in the self, hampered by the perception that their dark view of life is the only reality. After a time, when these people have experienced the quiet, consistent, unjudging empathy of the therapist, they begin to show the first signs of empathy themselves. They acquire the ability to move outside themselves and make the lovely discovery that the human condition is universal, that the others in their lives can be understood, that they themselves have much in common with them. And in the light of that discovery, their fears and suspicions are virtually dispelled. This comes as a revelation to them, with all its accompanying joy.

Some years ago I did a course in psychodrama, intending to deal with a dark facet of my own character. It helped me to do that, but it did much more. I think I learned more about empathy in that six-week course than in all the rest of my life. Under skilful direction I saw people use their imaginations to dramatise deeply painful events in their lives. In the therapeutic situation, they changed places with an estranged parent, an alienated sibling, a friend who had betrayed them, even with themselves at an earlier stage of their lives, to look at those destructive events from the other's point of view. And in the process, I saw people being reconciled with the one they had seen as the enemy, the one who had hurt them, the one whose actions they had thought they could never understand. Some, like me, were simply reconciled with themselves. I came away wondering why the church, which offers its members the beautiful sacrament of reconciliation, has not

yet taken much apparent interest in the science of psycho-
therapy, which is entirely dedicated to healing and reconciliation. But then the church has always tended more towards
the cerebral. We are defined as Catholics primarily because
we espouse the doctrines of the church with our minds. It's
only in recent times that we've begun to sing about the Lord
of the Dance.

It's fortunate for all of us that there is one place where the
imagination is considered legitimate, acceptable and even necessary, and that is in our enjoyment of the arts, be it literature,
the theatre, films, TV plays, music, dance, mime (of which it
is the very essence), sculpture, painting, clowning. It is through
art more than any other medium that we learn how to practise
empathy. As we get 'lost' in a book or a film, for instance, we
are unconsciously empathising with other people. We are
outside ourselves. We are standing in their shoes. How else
could we come to be laughing aloud at the humour of their
situations, cringing at their humiliations, fearing for their safety,
shedding tears in public for their sorrow? This is much deeper
than sympathy. We are weeping for the 'other' because, for that
space of time, we *are* the other. Our own anxieties and sorrows
are completely forgotten and, when it is over, we have to come
back to ourselves, blinking and momentarily disoriented. That
is empathy. If we can carry even a fraction of that understanding and identification out into the reality of our own world, the
'other' will never quite be the 'other' again.

Art can dissolve such corrosive parasites as prejudice and
superiority and contempt. When I am watching a play or
reading a book, I am not saying to myself, 'I'm a Catholic and
she's a Protestant' or 'I'm a woman and he's a man' or 'She's
black and I'm white'. I am not saying, 'I have nothing in
common with her' or 'I'm removed from this person who is a
Mormon or a homosexual or a Samoan or an Australian or
black or male'. Far from it. Once we are immersed in any given
character all those exterior differences become quite irrelevant.

We experience the one fundamental identification — our shared humanity. It is a union of the spirit, even when the other person is a character of fiction. The saints managed to translate this kind of empathy into their everyday relationships; more than anything else, that's what made them saints. And they were able to do so because, through their prayer and contemplation and their own intimate relationship with God, they had come to know that this is precisely how God relates to every human being.

It is in the reading of a book, more than in any other form of art, that we are given what is referred to as this 'God view'. A book has the leisure and the capacity to take us right inside the other person. Their secret inner life, so like our own, is laid out before our eyes: their jealousies and loves, their fears, hopes, weaknesses, strengths, their capacity for darkness and sin and their capacity for transparency and goodness. And when we recognise the presence of real evil in a character, we are given the insight by which to recognise our own hidden potential for evil. And our hidden potential for good.

Shakespeare, surely, gives us the truest, most brilliant canvas of what it means to be human. Our own lives may be painted within a smaller frame but we can still explore, in the tragedy of Macbeth, the havoc caused by our own immoderate ambition; it's our own damaging procrastination and indecisiveness that we perceive in Hamlet; and King Lear reflects back to us all too clearly the image of our own arrogance and lack of empathy. And when it comes to mindless conflict, we have the heartbreaking tragedy of Romeo and Juliet.

But if, for some reason, we don't read Shakespeare, then how about Graham Greene? No one in modern literature has gone to such lengths to take us deep into the heart of every 'other'. And, in doing so, he was always severely criticised, generally by both sides. He was never black or white enough. In the 1950s Greene sinned against all the political correctness of the time by being incapable of seeing the monster that was supposed to be hidden in every Communist. The McCarthyites hated him for it. But then he did not have enough single-minded conviction to suit the Communists either. He was despised by agnostics for being a Catholic and condemned by the church, which suspected he was an agnostic. His morality was dubious — too many shades of grey!

It was just too near the bone that he made one his most memorable characters a man of such frailty that he relied heavily on the whisky bottle and was yet a good and loving priest. It was not surprising that, in *The Power and the Glory*, Greene took us into his confidence about how he himself perceived every 'other' in his life: 'When you visualised a man or a woman carefully,' he wrote, 'you could always begin to feel pity . . . When you saw the corners of the eyes, the shape of the mouth, how the hair grew, it was impossible to hate. Hate was just a failure of the imagination.'

All of Greene's novels are arguments against this concept of hate and therefore against the whole notion of enmity. It has been said that each of his books is an essay on fallenness. But, in his feeling for the ambiguity of life, in his perception of its paradoxes, in his refusal to see people as black or white, in his lifelong endeavour to understand every position, he seems to challenge the Christian concept of forgiveness. Forgiveness works from the premise that one is right and the other wrong. Then the one who is right forgives the other. It is something that we do *to* another. Greene, though, seems to be saying that that kind of forgiveness is the prerogative of God alone, the only one who knows enough to forgive. He does not talk much about forgiveness between human beings. He insists that our enemies are every bit as frail and vulnerable as we are.

What remains for me in my broken relationships is not so much to forgive, as to be reconciled with the other. And that means being reconciled with myself at the same time. I'm inclined to think that is what God had in mind when he asked us to forgive our enemies.

10 Where to Start?

I find it one of the most beautiful experiences in life to come on this kind of forgiveness embodied in a human person. And it is equally moving to find that this weary old world, which thinks it has seen everything, has still the discernment and the humility to pay homage to such goodness. Te Whiti, the great pacifist Maori chief of Taranaki, was such a person. Gandhi of India was another and so were Martin Luther King and his wife, Coretta, in the United States. And, on the world stage today, people like Aung San Suu Kyi of Burma and Nelson Mandela of South Africa give us the continuing proof that such shining magnanimity is possible.

It is interesting that Mandela, who has so much to forgive his former enemies, never seems to use that word. He speaks rather of reconciliation between the peoples of South Africa. It suggests to me that his level of empathy is such that he actually *understands* white South Africans. Sometimes I feel I can discern in him a hidden compassion and pity for them. It's as though he can see what a mess they're in. They placed all their hope in the belief of their own racial superiority and, under the name of apartheid, they embodied it in the laws of South Africa. They held Mandela and his people in such contempt that they felt free to reduce them to the depths of degradation and poverty. He, of all people, should feel he has the right to say, 'I forgive you.' Yet he speaks only of reconciliation between the blacks and their white sisters and brothers. Mandela has a short temper, I believe, and no doubt he has other attributes that keep him firmly earthed in the human race, but he knows the priceless secret of forgiveness.

But when we think of enemies being reconciled, perhaps

after centuries of hostility, we cannot make reconciliation into a denial of past injustice. One side has inflicted serious hurt on the other: that needs to be acknowledged and a public apology made. And then the work of amending past harm has to be taken to its limit. On a recent Holy Thursday in Dublin a liturgy was held in the cathedral of the Church of Ireland in which the Archbishop of Canterbury asked pardon for the 'crass insensitivity' and 'dominating attitudes' of his people in dealing with the people of Ireland. At another point in the liturgy, other church leaders went from their places to wash the feet of men and women from the other side of the conflict, whose family members had been killed. Before all present, they expressed their sorrow and embraced. It was a moving piece of symbolism, but we must never forget that the place for reparation is out in the world. The symbolism of sorrow without reparation is worthless. Those who have inflicted injustice must not only repent but repair. We don't need to go outside Aotearoa New Zealand to know the truth and the urgency of that.

I often wonder what we would say of Jesus if he returned to earth. His empathy with others was such that it trapped him in very risky situations and ensured that he made lasting enemies. To give just one instance, let's take the occasion when a questioner asked him to define the term 'neighbour'. Jesus, answering by way of a parable, set up the following scenario. There was this victim of a severe mugging lying on the side of the road 'half dead'. Two of his countrymen passed by on the other side of the road, both Temple servants, the one a Levite and the other a priest. Both ignored the dying man. Jesus didn't condemn them, but simply stated that they passed by; he had empathy with them too. They failed the test of love, but he knew that they feared being rendered liturgically unclean if they touched the victim and, as a result, would not be able to carry out their Temple duties. They were the slaves of law.

He then introduced another character into the drama, a traveller on the same road, this time a Samaritan. He could just as easily have made this traveller a well-disposed Jew of the same ethnic and religious background as the victim. It would still have made his point effective. But he chose to make him a Samaritan, whom the Jews hated and despised. And it was this Samaritan who tended his wounded enemy with care and tenderness. That parable was bitter medicine for Jesus' listeners. We get an idea of just how bitter, when he asked his original questioner which character in the story did he consider had been a neighbour to the dying man. The Jew could not bring himself even to utter the word, Samaritan. He said instead, 'I suppose it was the one who ministered to him.' The one, indeed — the 'other'.

If Jesus were telling that parable to Croatian Christians today, he would script a dying Croat on the side of the road and a Croatian priest averting his face and leaving him there. And he would have said that the one who tended him was a Serb. To the Tutsi it would have become the parable of the Good Hutu and to a Catholic audience in Belfast it would have been a Protestant. He was defining the term 'neighbour', but he was taking it much further: he was saying that we can find our neighbour in the one we see as the enemy or the 'other'. But, to embrace that truth, we have first of all to be open to the hated 'other'. The little group of Catholics in Lurgan that day, once they had the opportunity to meet those three Protestants and hold their hands, knew that they were good people. They could no longer think of them as the enemy.

There is a strong connection between empathy and justice; they are full sisters. In 1981 in Aotearoa New Zealand we were completely polarised by a single issue. There were those who believed that we should demonstrate our abhorrence of apartheid in South Africa by refusing to play rugby with its perpetrators. And there were those who simply could not understand why we should poke our noses into the affairs of another country. Families, friends, even spouses found themselves divided, and people were bewildered and upset that it should be so. They found it difficult to explain why they felt as they did when someone close to them felt the opposite. I believe that the answer was to be found in imagination and empathy. Some could actually enter into the experience of the South African blacks, could imagine what it was like to live in the shacks of Soweto without the ordinary decencies of life. They could also imagine the affluence and luxury of the white sector. They had the measure of the gap. They could *feel* what it would be like to be forbidden by law to sit on a certain park bench, swim at this beach, travel in this bus, use this telephone box, marry this person. They looked at people like Bishop Tutu, denied the right to vote, and felt the outrage of it. And, in their empathy with the blacks, they knew themselves to be diminished as human beings in the degradation of the other. They needed to do what they could to bring about change.

If we are serious about nourishing the imagination so that we can step into the other person's shoes, get inside them and begin to understand their perception of life, there is one thing we should avoid like the proverbial plague. From my vantage point of three score years and thirteen, I've come to fear it almost obsessively. I believe that it might well be one of the tiny seeds, sown at the beginning, which causes the human conflict that so bewilders and exasperates us night after night. I am speaking of the racial joke, the ethnic, the religious, the gender, the xenophobic joke. Here lies danger. The joke is a seductive cover for the most sinister form of stereotyping.

Once we have a perception that another group of people is different from us, we begin to harbour a secret fear of them. And we try to diminish them, and to counter our fear, by making fools of them. It can always be made to seem innocuous because, when challenged, we can claim that 'it's only a joke'. It generates laughter. What harm could that possibly do? The answer is, plenty. So can name-calling. It's no coincidence that present-day Serbs call all Croatian fighters Ustase. That was the name of the Croatian fascist minority during the Second World War. And the Croats call the Serbs Chetnik, the name of the Serbian fascists a generation ago. Throughout my own child-hood in the years after the First World War, people were still talking darkly about 'the Huns' and I knew I never wanted to meet a German. A whole nation was classified as barbarian in the mind of a child.

In my lifetime, too, I can remember what were known as the Hori jokes. Hori, the symbol of every male Maori, was lazy, incompetent, unintelligent, brown and slightly inane — the stereotype of every Maori as the Pakeha wanted to see him. At the same time, we all believed that the two races in Aotearoa New Zealand lived in perfect harmony with each other, that it was acceptable to declare the Maori honorary whites so that they could play rugby in South Africa. They were bad days for our country when we were telling Hori jokes, and I've lived to see the day when few Pakeha would dare to tell them again. If that is what is meant by political correctness, I'm ready to defend it to my last breath. If it is political correctness that has robbed the dominant partner of the power to distort humour into a weapon of derision, then I believe in it, whether in reference to Maori, to women, to newly arrived immigrants, to beneficiaries or whoever else.

I hope I live to see the day when it will be politically in-correct to tell stereotyping jokes about Australians. Given time, the stereotype becomes just too hard to break. I remember once hearing someone quote a sociologist who had said, 'Never argue with a stereotype. It is more powerful than reality.' That's the truth of it. I don't want a child here to grow up on a diet of Australian jokes, without the judgment or the maturity to discern that the people across the Tasman do not differ from us except in a few minor inessentials. And don't tell me I haven't got a sense of humour. I love humour and prize it as one of the most precious of all human attributes.

But I not only prize humour, I respect its power. We could

well ponder to what extent jokes about Jews played a part in the final making of an anti-Semitic nation. What were the latest Muslim jokes before it became necessary to kill them off? We could well reflect on how the imagination can be drip-fed a certain stereotype about another group, passed on over generations, until we have lost the capacity to think outside it. The travesty has become the conviction, the stereotype the reality. Of course the joke cannot be held responsible for all the senseless brutality of one group against another but I think that for us, as we wring our hands uselessly in front of our TV screens, it would not be a bad starting point.

We may well be able to do something in our personal lives to head off disastrous divisions in the future of Aotearoa New Zealand. We have only to look at a small child to know that we must. But it remains difficult to keep alive the spirit of hope that the whole world will one day be healed and reconciled. Wars escalate, new hatreds are unleashed. Countries we had never heard of suddenly break into the news to reveal that they have been splintered for centuries by racial or tribal bitterness. I had never heard of the Tutsis or the Hutus before they began systematically wiping each other off the earth; I knew virtually nothing about Rwanda. But if it isn't Rwanda, it will be somewhere else. We begin to think there is no wisdom left in all the world. Abba Eban, a former foreign minister of Israel, sounded infinitely weary when he said, 'Men and nations behave wisely, once they have exhausted all other alternatives!' Sometimes, when I feel a wave of hopelessness breaking over me, I fear he may have got it right.

But my whole Christian life is as dependent on hope as it is on faith, so hope I must. Hope is sometimes expressed as a kind of optimism which is not really hope at all, because it chooses to ignore the ambiguity of human existence. And it sometimes is expressed as apathy, which sees no point in doing anything in the face of evil. All true hope, Christian or not, is grounded in reality and reality contains evil, much of it of our own making. We may, in ignorance or blasphemy, blame God for terrible famines that have their source in the greed, exploitation and disruption caused by powerful nations. Or for devastating floods caused by our destruction of trees that were destined to hold the earth secure. Or for the spoliation of creation by nuclear testing. Or for wars that have grown from the unchecked hatreds of centuries. We need honestly to acknowledge our part in the evil of the world. But there are also sorrows that are not of our own making: the unexplained death of the young, the pain of disability, sickness of the mind, unrequited love. These are all part of the human condition. And, if we are to hope, we have to hope in the midst of this reality. We have no other.

Ernest Bloch said that hope arises out of the human capacity to experience 'the not yet' of life, the conviction that, within our own lives and within humanity, there is still an unrealised potential. It was the theologian Karl Barth who said that hope is action, and it was Saint Augustine who said that Hope has two beautiful daughters, Anger and Courage: Anger at the way things are and Courage to change them. Only when we have empathy with others and solidarity with all humankind will we commit our energies to the promotion of goodness, the struggle for justice, the demand for human rights, the care of the earth, a commitment to social and political reform, the pursuit of happiness. Hope is the midwife of a future that we can help create.

Christian hope embraces all these aspects of hope, because a hope that neglects the wellbeing of the world is not Christian. But Christian hope has one added dimension: it is based on the preaching and the example of Jesus and it places his death and resurrection at its centre. I have to recognise that suffering and death are an intrinsic part of my existence. But, for me, there is no other way. My Christian hope resides in a Christ who was crucified. This historical reality leads me to embrace both darkness and light, tragedy and transformation, sadness and joy, death and resurrection as integral to my life. For me, hope is a bright darkness.

Fifteen years after our visit to Northern Ireland the movement for reconciliation and peace rose to the surface. It is still struggling to be earthed there, but beacons of light are beginning to glow through the darkness, the tragedy is receding, the transformation has begun, sadness is beginning to give way to joy, and the grave where death has triumphed for so long is breaking open to a resurrection.

11 Making History

If there was one event that was truly historical during that 1979 sojourn in the northern world, it was the Pope's visit to Ireland. It was the first time in the long history of the church that a Pope had ever been to that country, which had given unqualified loyalty to the papacy over centuries. But now, Pope John Paul II was going to set foot on Irish soil: Karol Wojtyla, a son of Poland, a country that had much in common with Ireland, that had known what it was to suffer under foreign oppression.

We were staying with a friend, Maureen Murphy, in a suburb of Dublin. Maureen had worked for many years as an educational psychologist in the Dublin area and had facilitated our study of community-based projects in that city. Now, with typical kindness and generosity, she had offered us the hospitality of her home so that we could participate in this momentous event. And what an event it was. All Ireland was abuzz with anticipation. Aer Lingus, the national airline, had handed out special treats, believing that its passengers had only one reason for coming to Ireland at that time; it seemed to be the only topic of conversation on buses and every interview on TV had something to do with the preparations, the itinerary, the public expectation. Everyone we met automatically assumed that we'd come for the sole purpose of 'seeing the Pope'. The air was impregnated with festivity, excitement and religious fervour.

The Pope was due to arrive on 29 September, early autumn in the Northern Hemisphere, and everyone was anxious about the weather. As well they might be! The weather in Ireland is scarcely to be trusted. But the night before the visit began the sky was ablaze with stars and not a sign of rain to be seen anywhere. The next morning Maureen called us at 4.30 and proceeded to carry out the preparations with the quiet flair of a born organiser. She had other guests besides us: her sister Pat with her fifteen-year-old son, Cormac, who had come from Cork. We made sandwiches enough for an army in combat, we had a breakfast designed to sustain us in the event of any unforeseen circumstance, we were allotted our respective chairs to carry and, at six o'clock on the dot, we trooped out onto the street to begin our march on Phoenix Park more than six kilometres away.

It was still dark, but the whole city was alive. Shadowy figures were streaming out of every front gate as we passed by, everyone talking, everyone greeting one another as they met in the dark. No one was a stranger in Dublin that morning. And as each house emptied out along the way we became part of a moving throng walking along beside the canal, all heading for the one destination. Everyone was on foot. Except for special cases, no buses or cars were permitted within eight kilometres of the park. We had a sense of a whole city setting out on a unique pilgrimage. And we were part of it!

Everyone had an air of jauntiness and light-heartedness, an expectation and joy that were almost tangible. As we walked along, the first signs of light began to streak the sky and our companions in the crowd were gradually transformed from faceless silhouettes into laughing, chattering, excited human beings. There were flags everywhere: the papal flag, the Irish flag, the clan flag with its emblem and motto proudly held aloft. We walked shoulder to shoulder stretched across footpaths and road with no vehicles to impede our progress. No one tried to outstrip anyone else, everyone kept an even pace. We had plenty of time: the Pope had not yet left Rome. I'm no great walker and six kilometres would normally stretch my capabilities, but not on this occasion. I felt as though I was being carried along on a warm, good-humoured, weightless tide of people. I could have walked double the distance. But the best was yet to come. At the exact moment that we arrived at the gates of Phoenix Park, converging with wave on wave of other people coming from all directions, the whole scene became suffused in a golden burst of light. It was sunrise!

Over a million people streamed into Dublin's huge park that day and to disperse them effectively over the specified area was a task of monumental proportions. But the organisation was breathtakingly good. A large section of the park was divided into 'corrals'. As we came through the nearest gateway we were allotted our particular corral, directed to its location and given its number. We were also provided with other relevant information, including how to get to the nearest cluster of Port-a-Loos that were set up around the park, looking for all the world like small orderly townships. Once within our corral we were to stay there for the rest of the day. The corral was exactly that — an enclave about two metres high with sturdy log uprights and only about three rows of log cross-beams providing strong parameters and allowing plenty of viewing space. Each one was designed to hold some two hundred people with room to move around, set up chairs, form into groups and begin eating. The atmosphere was pure carnival.

We had at least a four-hour wait before the Pope was due to arrive. And without a break over that whole time there was a steady stream of people going past. There were hundreds of other corrals to fill, and, as trains and buses converged on Dublin from the surrounding counties, masses of people continued to pour in. To the forest of waving flags was now added a colourful variety of banners proclaiming the county of origin of each group of pilgrims. The Pope was to visit three other venues in Ireland during the next couple of days, but Dublin drew nearly a third of the whole population.

From time to time, I stood up on the tall kitchen stool-cum-ladder that Maureen had thoughtfully assigned to me for the day and looked out over the surrounding park. I turned full circle and, for as far as the eye could absorb on every side, there was nothing to be seen but the tops of human heads. In the end I stopped looking. There was something vaguely frightening about being enclosed within such a multitude of people. But there were endless distractions. By now the Pope was well on his way. We followed his journey across Europe and the voice on the speaker system even ventured to confide to us what he was possibly thinking. But we were on much firmer ground when we were told what he was having for breakfast: eggs, bacon, tomatoes, black pudding . . . the rest was drowned out by a concerted groan and the collective response was to open up the picnic baskets and begin eating again!

As the moment of his arrival grew closer, a hush fell over the concourse and every head was turned upwards to the waiting sky. Suddenly the huge plane came into sight. It will remain one of the most unforgettable moments of my life. The Aer Lingus plane was a great white bird with wing plumage of deepest green and blue, against an azure noon sky, cloudless and clear. It flew low over Phoenix Park, no doubt to give the Pope a bird's-eye view of the scene below. It's hard to imagine what it must have looked like from above — a vast sea of faces lifted in welcome — but I certainly know what I felt like on the ground. In that instant every bit of Irish history I ever knew was present to me, every myth, every poem, every folk story, every ballad, every song. And all of it sad. And it was sad in great part because of this man and his predecessors and everything that their office represented. Because if the Irish had been prepared to abandon their allegiance to the Roman Catholic church, and to reject the authority of the Pope, things could have been very different. Instead, they chose alienation from their rulers, poverty, powerlessness, ridicule, hunger, eviction, exile. Denied education, they learned to read furtively in hedge-schools; forbidden the practice of their religion, they worshipped as fugitives; barely literate, they recorded their history in song; robbed of the ownership of their land, they became destitute tenants at best and degraded labourers at worst. And finally, when their lives were in too great danger from persecution or hunger or homelessness, they had no option but to make their way to the nearest port and travel in indescribable conditions to the other side of the world.

But throughout it all, the suffering, the degradation, the alienation, there had always been one positive constant — their faith. And, with it, their loyalty to the Pope. As the plane carrying 'himself' flew low overhead, a great cry of welcome went up from a million throats. I was, in those few minutes, filled with an emotion of such power and intensity that my body had great difficulty containing it, my limbs were trembling and my breath coming in short gasps. As the plane moved in a downward glide to the airport and disappeared from view, the bubble of other-consciousness in which I had been completely enclosed suddenly broke and I stepped out into the reality of my immediate world. In that moment I became aware that Donald Malloch, who was arguably the only Presbyterian minister in all that crowd, had tears pouring down his face.

After that heart-stopping emotional climax, as the events of the rest of the day unfolded, I found myself taking on more and more the role of an observer and setting a distance between me and what I, a visitor from another country, was experiencing. A helicopter brought the pontiff from the airport to the park and he was escorted to the great white altar with its tall pillars and its waving flags, far too distant for us to make out the people gathered there. In a blur of clerical blacks and whites and bishops' purples and cardinals' reds we could discern a lone figure in white. Or we thought we could.

Later, the newly designed popemobile was driven along the intricate maze of grassy roads through the corrals so that it passed slowly at the side of every one of them. By an extraordinary piece of organisation every single person in Phoenix Park that day came within a few metres of the Pope as he made his unhurried passage through their midst, his broad Slav face beaming with delight as he blessed them and waved and blessed them again, the sons and daughters of Ireland.

By the time the Mass began our corral was already a community. Even though the progress of the Mass was relayed over an impeccable speaker system it still remained a challenge to everyone's piety to stay with what was happening on the great white altar in the distance. The scene became a wonderful blending of the sacred with the secular. Animated conversations with newly made friends were reverently suspended during the words of consecration, only to be taken up again as soon as the moment was over. The Irish have always blurred the lines between the practice of their faith and the living of their daily lives. Their everyday conversation is peppered with prayer as they thank God for the good things and ask for help with the difficult, with not the slightest break in the narrative. It was only people like me who found it disconcerting. In countries like New Zealand we have so effectively separated the secular and the holy that to bring them together in public requires a deliberate act of courage and is, more often than not, decidedly self-conscious.

When it came time for Holy Communion the hosts were distributed by hundreds of priests fanning out over the park. By that time I was becoming too tired to reflect on the mystical implications of what was happening as a million people were united in the breaking and eating of that holy bread. I lined up with everyone else for Holy Communion, feeling less than devout, and when I should have been immersed in prayer I was instead marvelling at the magnitude of the logistics entailed in the whole exercise. A few moments after Communion everyone settled down to another meal and the festivity continued in a noisy and happy *agape*. I, for one, thought that the Mass must have been finished so it came as a shock to me when, after what must have been a full three-quarters of an hour, the speaker system burst into renewed life and the unmistakably inflected voice of the Pope said, 'Let us pray.' The distribution of Holy Communion had been going on all that time and the Mass was still in progress! But the party spirit continued unabated and no one was the least dismayed. It was all blended into one: the tidying up after the sacred meal at the altar and the packing up of the picnic baskets in the corral.

Things moved quickly after that. The Mass ended, words of farewell were spoken, last blessings were given, a helicopter buzzed importantly overhead and the Pope was whisked away. The day had been all that everyone expected it to be and a thousand times more. The sun was still shining when the process of emptying the park began. We were with friends who knew the way and we headed to the gate nearest to our side of the city. The historic day, memorable and momentous, was over.

12 Ten Years On

From time to time after my return to New Zealand I pondered what the Pope's visit had meant, especially to the Irish. At the time there had appeared to be virtually no analysis of the occasion. The Irish media had been caught up in the prevailing hype as much as everyone else. They obviously thought it was no occasion for thoughtful observations, let alone for any critical interpretation of such dazzling events. I used to wonder if that's how things had stayed. But, ten years later in 1989, out of the blue, Maureen Murphy sent me a video of a programme that had just been shown on Irish television, and I had my answer. The video was made up of interviews with various people in which they were asked for their thoughts on the papal visit from the perspective of a decade further on.

What most of them were saying in one way or another was that the Pope's visit hadn't made the slightest bit of difference to anything. One world-weary journalist admitted that many, like himself, had thought that his coming might effect some kind of spiritual regeneration for Ireland. He claimed that this had been a hope not only of conservative people but of contemporary, liberal Irish. These were the people enjoying all the attributes of modern materialism, yet uneasily aware of the corresponding degeneration of the spiritual life of their country. But the Pope, he said with an edge of bitterness in his voice, had offered them nothing except a return to their traditional ways. He had been as effective as King Canute commanding the tide to turn back on its course. They were forced to the conclusion that although, for a few magical days, the country had known glorious unity, this had merely masked their divisions rather than healed them. But, in retrospect, they had the

71

grace to acknowledge that they might have expected just a little too much of one human being.

One priest from Maynooth, a prestigious Irish seminary, likened the Pope's visit to Jesus entering Jerusalem on Palm Sunday and the delirious joy of the Jews as they placed palms beneath his feet. But that event in Jesus' life had been followed by all the sorrow, confusion and near-despair of the days we now call Holy Week. This priest believed that in the ten years between 1979 and 1989 the Irish had experienced a prolonged Holy Week of suffering. They'd had unrelenting war in the North, hunger strikes, violence and death, and, in the South, moving statues, weeping madonnas, bizarre visions — a wave of the worst extremes of religious devotion on the one hand and a tidal swell of religious scepticism on the other. He likened the decade to some dark trauma for the Irish psyche, a period of extraordinary depression economically, socially, culturally. Then, returning to the imagery of Palm Sunday, he finished by saying that for the decade after the Pope's visit the Irish were like people left with palms in their hands, not knowing what to do with them. They had hoped the papal visit was the beginning of something new, but it had proved to be an end of a way of believing, an end of the Catholic consensus in Ireland.

But the pain of the 1980s must have later seemed merely a curtain-raiser to what followed in the 1990s. The trauma was to intensify as one scandal after another erupted in quick succession. And the church was singularly unprepared to cope with them. Its leadership, it would appear, has not been able to move quickly enough from its traditional, clerical, privileged and powerful status to the very different kind of leadership needed to meet the contemporary needs of modern Ireland, a country that becomes more pluralistic and cosmopolitan by the day. In the past, the power wielded by the Irish hierarchy had always seemed unassailable. And this power had been used to bring to heel not only the laity and the minor clergy but even, on occasions, the government itself.

Such power politics had been most fully epitomised in the person of one John Charles McQuaid, long-time Archbishop of Dublin, reactionary, right wing and obdurate. He was appalled by the reforms of the Second Vatican Council, even though they had been passed with the fullest authority of the church. He would have none of it. On his return to Dublin after attending the Council in Rome he told his people, 'You may have been worried by much talk of changes to come. Allow me to reassure you. No change will worry the tranquillity of your lives.' But such disobedience to the church, which amounts to flagrant hostility to the movement of the Holy Spirit, comes only at a price. And that price is being exacted of the Irish church in the 1990s.

The first major scandal, and the one with the most far-reaching effects, was the revelation that the Bishop of Galway, Dr Eamonn Casey, was not only the father of a teenage son but had used church funds over many years for his support. Irish Catholics sat enthralled and stunned before their television sets as the bishop's former partner described their relationship. Here was a bishop who had undoubtedly been a great lover. He had also been a much-loved pastor. And he had been an urbane and gracious host to the Pope in the west of Ireland, where the papal injunction to the laity had been almost exclusively about sexual morality. Now the Irish people, reading their newspapers and watching their televisions, must surely have felt that they had reached a watershed in their relationship with the church and especially with its leaders.

The Irish of today are significantly different from what they were in the past. The new generations are now highly educated, oriented towards Europe and the United States, well travelled, increasingly feminist and, as they have always been, quick-witted and articulate. They are a force to be reckoned with; if the church does not provide credible leadership and give relevant answers to the questions of modern Ireland it runs a real risk of being increasingly ignored. This has also been shown to be true of the Irish government. If it is not open and upright in its actions it will be brought down, as former Prime Minister Albert Reynolds discovered to his cost in 1994. The man from Maynooth was right. The old way of believing and the old Catholic consensus has gone.

In the light of all this, what I witnessed that day in Phoenix Park was of far greater significance than I had ever dreamed. For me, at the time, it was an event bathed solely in the light of history. It was for the past that I had shed tears. But that day was to be just as significant for the future. The Pope's visit in September 1979 would be the benchmark from which the Irish would later measure their new relationship with the church. The outcome was not what they had expected. Instead of being drawn more deeply into the life of the church as they had always known it, they were to begin distancing themselves from it, standing a little way back, breaking with an unquestioning past to ask vital, new questions pertaining to their contemporary lives. And if they find no nourishment at the table there, they may well begin to walk away. That is the stuff of which history is made.

But it is much more than that. It is the stuff from which a deeper spiritual life is forged, the stuff that brings us into closer contact with Christ, who gave new answers to the people of his time and then suffered and died on their behalf. The Palm Sunday and Holy Week image that the Maynooth priest gave on the television programme was never without hope. And that might seem strange if we did not know that this is the path that Jesus followed, that it was through suffering that he came to triumph over evil: over systematic injustice, the unworthy use of power, the coercion of the human conscience, the exploitation of his beloved poor. He had to confront human sinfulness before he could triumph over it. And his sole motive was to give us access to his life by which we, too, can overcome both our petty, personal sinfulness and our forays into evil and, even

more painfully, our collective institutional sins of greed and ruthlessness towards the weak. It was not through the triumph of Palm Sunday that Jesus gave us eternal life. It was through his life struggle and the suffering of Holy Week which ended with his scandalous and shameful death. And from that death came his glorious resurrection to a new life — and we with him. The Irish church has every reason to be full of hope.

13 The Beginning of Siege

Each local church is, in one way or another, a microcosm of the universal church, and what is happening in Ireland is happening in varying degrees all over the world. What occurs in the church at any given time can never be viewed in isolation from the attitudes and actions of the Pope of that particular era. Take Pope John Paul II as a case in point: a man of such complexity, scholarship and stature that most other leaders seem to pale beside him. He is a Slav and, more than that, the particular breed of Slav that comes out of Poland — a country oppressed for centuries, partitioned and repartitioned, persecuted, humiliated, reduced to nothing, but never destroyed. And as the cycle of history came around yet again in the twentieth century, Karol Wojtyla in his lifetime experienced all these things happening to his beloved country and played a courageous and distinguished part in resisting them.

Such national suffering is a fire in which strong personalities are forged. In those people tough enough to survive, it sparks a unique spirit of self-confidence and self-reliance. And when these qualities are coupled with a profound faith in God, they can induce a certain feeling of invincibility, a belief that everything is possible if one is single-minded enough, forceful enough, astute enough, committed enough, persevering enough, passionate enough and, above all, if one prays enough. No mission is too daunting for such a person. And the mission that Pope John Paul II seems to have set himself is nothing less than to save the soul of the world — single-handed if necessary.

And it's precisely this particular aspect of the Pope's approach to his leadership that has had a marked impact on the church in recent times. When he speaks, he's not just any leader

— he's the Pope. And he speaks with such power, conviction and authority as to suggest that he must be obeyed under all circumstances. In the face of such certainty, and such serious and uncompromising injunctions, I have heard people asking anxiously, in classic Catholicese, 'Is the Pope speaking infallibly?' And remaining unsure if they can trust an elderly nun like me when she says, 'No!'

Their question has its roots in nineteenth-century history. Ever since the First Vatican Council in 1870, when the 'infallibility of the Pope' was made a doctrine of the church and therefore a matter of strict belief, great numbers of Catholics have remained relatively bemused about what it really means and under what circumstances it applies. The catechism of my youth told me that when the Pope spoke solemnly from the chair of Peter as supreme pastor, on faith or morals to be held by the whole church, he could not be mistaken. It was bald language, take it or leave it, but it was obvious to those who thought about it that an infallible decree could be expressed only within certain limits. And it was only in later years that I heard of the role that the Holy Spirit of God would play in all this, working through the whole People of God, lovingly protecting the church from the pitfalls of error and the danger of false teaching.

The folklore that developed was very different. Growing up, listening to Catholic talk around me, I got the distinct impression that papal infallibility meant that the Pope could never make a mistake. If the Holy Father said that something was evil, it was evil. And if the Holy Father said it was good, then it was good. It was a simple interpretation and it helped give Roman Catholics the comforting certainties and high security that they enjoyed until comparatively recently. There's little doubt that all this was made vastly easier by the fortuitous circumstance that, during my lifetime and that of my immediate forebears, the Popes have been good and holy men. We have had no Borgia Pope to put our trust in the Holy Spirit to any serious test! But even so, comforting as the belief may be, it is simply not correct. The church has never taught that every time the Pope speaks, he is incapable of error.

Even in my relatively short life, I have seen how the personality and background of the various Popes of my time had a profound effect on what transpired during their papacies. This has been illustrated in each of them: Pius XI, Pius XII, John XXIII, Paul VI, in the little we know of John Paul I and certainly in John Paul II. It has always been so, but never more than in the person of Pius IX, the Pope who took the long-held belief that the Holy Spirit would always protect the church from false teaching, and made it into a doctrine of the church to be embraced by everyone calling themselves Catholic. The burning question of that era, a hundred years ago, was: would the Holy Spirit be acting through the Pope alone or through the Pope acting in union with his bishops throughout the world? It is a question that has never gone away. What it asks is: was Jesus talking to all the Apostles when he promised to be with them until the end of time, or only to Saint Peter?

In considering the action of Pope Pius IX we have to realise also that papal actions can never be divorced from the world events in which they are set, be it the outbreak of the Second World War for Pius XII or the ascent of Nazism and Communism in Eastern Europe for John Paul II. For Pius IX in the nineteenth century it was the growth of liberalism and nationalism in Europe. His papacy, the longest in history, covered the years 1846 to 1878, a period that witnessed some of the most momentous events in modern history, events that laid the foundations for the freedoms and developments of our own era, as well as for its wars and regressions. Most of these events can be traced to the French Revolution of 1789, with its rallying cry of liberty, equality and fraternity and its sustained attack on oppressive power élites in both church and state. It had proclaimed the essential dignity of every human being and, as a natural consequence of that, the right of every person to equality and freedom.

Pius IX's papacy began just when liberalism was taking hold all over Europe, in the church as in every other walk of life. Percolating gradually through all society, it was especially strong in the new middle classes. People everywhere were entertaining utopian dreams of a world where they would no longer be under the heel of a foreign oppressor and where they would have some say in the affairs of their own country. It was a heady mix, this growing desire for nationalism and democracy. But when you added to that much talk about freedom of thought, freedom of speech, freedom of the press, freedom of assembly and freedom of religion — freedoms that were virtually non-existent in any society — you had a potent political cocktail. Rulers in every European country, whose thrones had been so recently restored to them after the ravaging exploits of Napoleon, sensed that their power was once again being threatened by these sweeping new ideas and ruthlessly opposed them. And few of them had been more inexorable in their opposition than Pius IX's predecessor, Pope Gregory XVI.

But the new Pope took a different stance and showed that he was not unaffected by the new liberal climate. His first papal actions were such that liberals everywhere could be forgiven for inferring that he was one of them. He began by declaring an amnesty for all political prisoners in the Papal States and went on to take the first tentative steps towards democracy by granting his subjects a constitution, the rainbow's end for every nineteenth-century liberal. This one provided the Papal States with a bicameral parliament elected by an indirect form of suffrage. The Pope, as the legitimate ruler, had the right of veto. Still, a constitution was a constitution.

Those leading the liberation movements in such countries as Germany, Austria, France, Belgium, Hungary and, of course, Italy itself were utterly delighted at this unexpected turn of events, while those seeking to maintain the status quo and hold back all possibility of change were horrified beyond belief. But whether delighted or horrified, both extremes were equally astounded at such an unlikely phenomenon. Metternich, foreign minister of the great Austrian Empire, implacably opposed to the forces of change, was the most percipient and powerful statesman in Europe at the time. Yet even he was caught unawares. 'We were prepared for everything except a liberal Pope,' was his shocked reaction. 'And now we have one, there is no answering for anything!'

Metternich need not have worried. Pius IX soon became caught up in a web of events that was far too complex for him to handle. In 1848, his new parliament voted to send papal troops to help drive out the Austrians who were occupying North Italy. The Pope, although he sympathised with Italian nationalism and shared the dream of a united Italy, felt he could not use his troops to fight Austria, a Catholic power with a long tradition of loyalty to the church. He used his veto. The troops were withdrawn and the anger and disappointment all around him was so high that riots broke out, his prime minister was assassinated and mobs surrounded the papal palace. Pius IX was forced to flee Rome in disguise and was able to return two years later only with the protection of French troops. It was a traumatic experience, and people have become reactionaries for far less. Any sympathy Pius IX had entertained for liberalism was now effectively extinguished and he became an uncompromising opponent of all change. More than anyone else, he was responsible for the siege mentality that beset the Catholic church for the hundred years before Pope John XXIII convened the Second Vatican Council in 1962.

Nothing could stem the tide of events, however. In the ten years between 1850 and 1860, Italy became virtually a united country — the Austrians had been driven out of most of the north, Garibaldi and his Red Shirts overthrew the cruel Bourbon rulers in the south. The latter then went straight on to join

north and south by conquering the Papal States, which strad-
dled central Italy. The Pope's temporal power was all but gone.
But the cool-headed Cavour of the north held the hot-headed
Garibaldi of the south from taking the city of Rome. He knew
that, if that happened, either France or Austria might enter the
fray to support the Pope, and their work in creating a united
Italy free of foreign rule could be lost. Instead Cavour offered
Pius IX a settlement which, in return for giving up his control
of the Papal States, would give him complete independence
and control over everything pertaining to the church, be it
teaching, education or the press, and provide a regular, agreed
income for the Papal Court, the Sacred College and the epis-
copate and clergy as a whole. The church was also to be con-
firmed in the ownership of all galleries, palaces and monu-
ments that it had traditionally held. It was a settlement not all
that dissimilar from the Lateran Treaty of 1929, which a later
Pope negotiated with Mussolini, giving independence to the
tiny Vatican State that Popes rule to this day.

But in 1860, Pius IX was too shattered by events and too
influenced by reactionary advisers to listen. He refused the
settlement and stayed on in Rome under the protection of the
French government. It was only a matter of time before Rome
fell. Italian nationalists could not bear the thought of the
ancient city not being the capital of their proud new state. The
moment came ten years later in 1870, when the Franco-
Prussian War broke out and France suddenly needed every one
of her soldiers in order to defend herself against the highly
efficient Prussian army. The French troops were recalled from
Rome and the Italian army immediately claimed the city. The
final step in making a united Italy was complete. Pius became,
in his own words, 'a prisoner of the Vatican'. But he was not
idle in his voluntary confinement. He saw what course events
would most likely take and, not without good reason, he feared
the growth of the secular nation state and its effect on the
church. His reaction was to use much of his long reign to

strengthen the power of the papacy within the church itself. He went about this in a thoroughly systematic way.

He extended tighter control over bishops and appointed only those who were in step with his anti-liberal views. He cultivated the loyalty of the lower clergy so that they were encouraged to look to the Pope for leadership rather than to their local bishop. He established national seminaries in Rome where young aspirants to the priesthood could be brought from all over the world to imbibe the Roman spirit at its source. Anyone who expressed dissent, be it bishop, priest or theologian, felt the heat of his wrath. In time, all Catholic eyes came to turn towards Rome as the effectual centre of the church and the role of the local church diminished proportionately. Things that would normally have been decided by the local church, with the benefit of local knowledge, now had to go to distant Rome for papal approval. In time it became acceptable, if you found yourself in disagreement with your local bishop, simply to go over his head and take your case directly to Rome.

Religious Orders, whose independence was often a thorn in the side of their bishops, found this particularly helpful and they flourished during this time. The Foundress of the Josephite Sisters, Mother Mary MacKillop, who was recently beatified in Australia, was such a one. Finding herself at serious odds with certain Australian bishops who wanted to control her work, she went to Rome. Sister Marie Therese Foale, in her history of the Josephite Order written in 1989 as a thesis for her PhD, makes this rather trenchant observation: 'When it listened to the representations of the members of this small, obscure religious community from a distant colony ahead of those made by their bishops, it seemed that Rome was concerned first and foremost for the sisters' welfare. However, another consideration . . . was its desire to maintain close control over the church in the colonies. From this point of view, the Josephites were little more than pawns in an episcopal power game and Rome's move to make them independent of the local bishops was an attempt to check those bishops' power.'

It was a development in the church that had its weaknesses as well as its strengths, and many within the church were alarmed at the exaltation of Rome at the expense of the local church and of the leadership of the Pope at the expense of that of the local bishop. Not everyone might have gone as far as the Archbishop of Rheims when he spoke of this 'idolatry to the papacy' but, for all that, there was widespread disquiet. This was not, however, shared by everyone. Church leaders were deeply polarised on the issue but the majority, for various reasons, supported the Pope. They felt that the traumatic loss of the Papal States, the last remnant of the secular power of the papacy, needed to be counterbalanced by the growth of its moral and spiritual power. And, given the speed and enormity of the changes taking place in the remaining thirty years of last century, they believed the church had good reason to become a strong fortress, protecting itself from the perceived evils of the modern world. Most bishops feared the new liberalism as a threat to the stability of the established order, they feared the arrogance and power of the recently established nation states, particularly in Italy and Germany, and, human nature being what it is, they feared what might happen to them if they opposed a Pope who had demonstrated little patience with dissidents.

14 Are Popes Always Right?

It was in this context that the doctrine of Infallibility was finally defined at the First Vatican Council in 1870. Pope Pius IX had already, in 1864, published his famous *Syllabus of Errors*, which constituted a defiant attack on 'the world' and on all forms of modern progress. Some of these 'errors' are still of universal concern: his condemnation of the socialism that subjects the individual and the family to the total power of the state, and his equally strong condemnation of the liberal capitalism that gives the same kind of unfettered power to the marketplace. But the *Syllabus* was compiled in such a complicated and clumsy way that it read as an unqualified condemnation of every modern development up to that time, including the new liberal concepts of freedom of religion and separation of church and state. Most Catholics prefer not to be reminded of it and, mercifully, its more excessive aspects were quietly abjured ninety years later at the Second Vatican Council.

The actual passing of the decree on infallibility took place in the midst of passionate debate. The bishops of the world were split on the issue. The core difference of opinion between the two factions was whether infallibility was vested in the Pope alone, or only when the Pope acted in consultation with all the bishops of the world, as happens, for instance, at a Council of the Church. Pius IX and the majority of the bishops favoured the former, and that is what was finally passed. Some sixty bishops, when they saw what way things were going, would have no part of it and, before the vote was taken, they withdrew from the Council. Later, when the decree was passed, they had to face a severe struggle of conscience about accepting it. In the end, all the dissident bishops submitted, consoling themselves that, in the course of the debate, they had prevented the decree from becoming too extreme and trusting that future councils would rectify its more exaggerated claims.

For all that, it remained a triumph for the forces of absolutism and a bitter blow to those who had hoped to see the Catholic church affirming democratic development and the modern progress of humanity in the nineteenth century. Not least, the decree also acquired the dubious honour of being one of the most misunderstood of all church teachings. But the official church of the time had seen the whole process as a way of protecting the papacy and the church everywhere from the overweening power of the state, a fear which, in the light of twentieth-century history, was not altogether misplaced. Perhaps the minority of bishops who opposed the decree in the form that it took would have been consoled had they known that it has been used only once since then. In 1950, the traditional Catholic belief that Mary, the mother of Jesus, was after her death assumed body and soul into Heaven, was declared by Pope Pius XII to be a dogma of the church. No other Pope has formally invoked infallibility.

The First Vatican Council ended in disarray, not only because of what was happening inside it, but because of what was happening outside. No matter how the church might try to closet itself from the world, the world has an unfortunate habit of intruding. It was July 1870: Rome was about to become Italy's once again and the Pope was left with nothing to rule except the church itself. The traumatic effect on Pius IX of the loss of his temporal power, and especially the loss of Rome, is scarcely credible in our time. But it does reveal the degree to which the church had seen its temporal power as an essential means of safeguarding its independence. Sadly, it also revealed its reliance on the majesty and magnificence of the papal mystique to give weight to its decrees. I don't think we fully perceived how deeply symbolic it was that both Pope John Paul I and Pope John Paul II did away with the solemn crowning of Popes at their inauguration ceremony. They were giving decent burial to the idea, already dead, that the papacy is a monarchy.

In the midst of all the danger and upheaval of the forcible taking of Rome in 1870, prudence dictated that the bishops assembled there for the Council get out as fast as their dignity and available transport permitted. The Pope adjourned the Council *sine die*, and it is of profound importance that its agenda was not nearly covered. Had the First Vatican Council been able to take its course, there would have been debate on and some resolution of the role of bishops, and particularly of the relationship of bishops to the Pope in the teaching ministry of the church. But that had not taken place and, needless to say, there had been no discussion on the role of the clergy nor of the laity, the ordinary men and women who make the church a reality. It is significant that, until recently, they have had to be content with being defined, not by what they are, but by what they are not. They are lay in the sense that they are not clergy.

The People of God — that is how the laity were defined at the Second Vatican Council, which met in 1962. Vatican II, called by Pope John XXIII, was as positive in its outlook as Vatican I had been negative, especially in its approach to the modern world. It showed a real desire to listen to what the world had to say to the church. Far from condemning progress, Pope John believed that God's action pulsated through the trends and movements of the modern world and that the Holy Spirit spoke through the people who inhabited it. The Second Vatican Council spoke freely of the church's love of people and its divine destiny to be the servant of humankind. This spirit was not all due to the benign personality of Pope John — it was the considered response of the church in general — but his personality had a lot to do with it. He was the inspiration that released all this pent-up desire to express love rather than fear, to use, in his words, the 'medicine of mercy' rather than the punishment of condemnations and bans, and to see sin as a sickness, a lack of wholeness that needs healing much more than it needs punishment. As for the term, People of God, it was the oldest, indeed the original, title of Christ's church. It was Saint Peter who said, 'You are now God's people!' (1 Peter 2:10). That is the fundamental concept whereby the church interprets and understands itself. If it is not the People of God, it is nothing.

Vatican II, without external disruptions, was able to cover its entire agenda. One of its most outstanding achievements was that it wrote a constitution for the church, something that had never been done before in all its long history. The constitution began by describing the role, not of the Pope, not of the hierarchy, not of the clergy, but of the People of God. It was a long overdue acknowledgment that it is the people, consecrated by Baptism, who are the primary constituents of the church. So how was the role of the papacy seen in 1962? It remained as intact and essential as ever, but there was now a moral obligation that it should no longer be exercised in the style of an absolute monarch and that the church should return to government by the whole college of bishops with the Pope at their head. And the bishops? They were defined as teachers and witnesses of faith, united with one another, and at one with their people. The beautifully inclusive word employed to express all this was co-responsibility. The bishops consult with and listen to their people. The Pope consults with and listens to his bishops. That is how the Holy Spirit acts in the church. And that, essentially, is how the church will be preserved from error.

Although Pope John Paul II appears to have lifted the profile of the papacy to new heights during his regime, he has never used the word infallible' to support his statements. They can be described as strong and passionate and authoritative, but not infallible — not in the sense that the church defines that term. In his book, *Crossing the Threshold of Hope*, where he comes as close as he's likely to get to revealing his inner self, he makes it clear that his attitudes are fully in accord with those of the Second Vatican Council, not the First. His interviewer, Vittorio Messori, put to him the question of how a sinful human being could claim to be the Vicar of Christ on earth. In his reply, John Paul II speaks of himself as the successor of Saint Peter. (He could have explained to his questioner that the title was, for centuries, not Vicar of Christ, but Vicar of Peter, from the Latin 'vicarius', meaning a substitute.) But if he did not discount the term Vicar of Christ, he did point out that he was the successor of Peter, the apostle who sinned to the extent of denying that he ever knew Jesus. For all that, it was in Peter that Jesus, after his resurrection, invested the leadership of the Apostles and promised that he would be with them until the end of time. Peter became the rock, as the Pope said, 'even if as a man, perhaps, he was nothing more than shifting sand'.

But what is most significant in his reply is that John Paul sets the papacy firmly in the context of its unity with the bishops, who are, in their turn, the successors of the Apostles. Certainly, he tells us, the title Vicar of Christ teaches of Christ's personal presence in the person of the Pope. But, he insists, it is not only the Pope who holds this title. Every Christian is 'another Christ' and every bishop in his diocese a Vicar of Christ. So, to use his own words, the real meaning of the Pope's title cannot be considered 'apart from the dignity of the entire college of Bishops'. He goes even further by saying: 'On reflection, *christianus* has greater significance than *episcopus*, even if the subject is the Bishop of Rome'.

Well might the Pope say that to be a Christian is of greater significance than to be a bishop. But it does not always appear easy for either Pope or bishop to accept this in practice and to recognise that the Holy Spirit may choose to give insights and wisdom to the ordinary Christian that are not given to the bishop or even to the Pope. If the leaders of the church really did accept this truth, they would surely show themselves more ready to listen to the women and men who make up the body of the church and there would not be the all too evident and manifest distrust of the views of lay people, especially those who dare to disagree, seen in the church today. This inability to listen to the people exposes the church to a danger from within that no enemy from without could possibly inflict.

I remember pondering all this some years ago when I read in the English *Tablet* an extract of the minutes of a March 1939 meeting between the cardinals of Germany and Pope Pius XII. This meeting took place not long after the papal election and in the same month that Hitler invaded Austria, just six months before the outbreak of the Second World War. It is clear that the background and personality of Pius XII was an important factor in the events portrayed in those minutes. Holy, scholarly, cautious and urbane, and by training a professional diplomat, he wanted to offer the German leader the courtesy of a letter announcing his election as Pope. He did not like the Nazis but, for the sake of the church in Germany, he wanted to make this gesture of goodwill at the outset of his pontificate. So here he was consulting the heads of the church in Germany. He needed their advice and he was listening to them.

I believe they failed him. One of the many complex reasons for this could well have been that they were too distanced from their people to hear what they might have been saying. The minutes of that meeting record that the Pope read to the cardinals the draft of his letter to Hitler. It was written in Latin. Cardinal Faulhaber is recorded as saying, 'No definite wish can be expressed in a letter of this kind — only a blessing. But there's one point. Must it be in Latin? The Führer's very touchy about non-Germanic languages . . .' The decision was then taken to send the letter in both Latin and German. Then there was the question of how to address Hitler. Should it be 'Illustrious' or 'Most Illustrious'? Should it be in the plural or the singular? Here the minutes record the response of Cardinal Bertram. 'I'm glad you haven't referred to him as *dilecte fili* (beloved son). He wouldn't appreciate that. (Joking) He'd like the Holy Father to cry, Heil, Heil!'

But what was the reality of life for the German people when this meeting was taking place? History tells us of the awful events that had been increasing in ferocity over the previous five years, and that were rampant by 1939: the Jews were being rounded up and sent to concentration camps, the dreaded SS troops were terrorising all those who opposed the Führer, the press was muzzled, all non-Nazi organisations, including political parties and trade unions, were abolished. The cardinals must surely have been aware of these things. But who in the church would have been most painfully aware of them? Who would have been actually experiencing them in one form or another in their daily lives? Surely it was the people living next door to the Jews whose property was confiscated and who mysteriously disappeared. It was the family whose son had been a trade unionist. It was the wife of the journalist who had been silenced.

There seems little doubt now that there was plenty of support for Hitler among German Catholics. He played his cards with consummate cunning. He knew that the church was obsessed with fear of Communism and that his policy of eliminating every Communist, 'the scum of the earth', and all traces of Communism itself from Germany would have a strong appeal, not only to the leaders of the church but to its members. He assessed with fair accuracy that it might even blind them to the profound immorality of his own policies. And, with equal astuteness, he saw that many in the church, and indeed in the whole of Germany, were secretly anti-Semitic.

Even so, not every German Catholic was anti-Jewish. Not every German man or woman was a Nazi. There were plenty of staunch church people who knew the full extent of what was going on in Germany in March 1939, people who, in Gospel terms, were 'the salt of the earth'. But did they have any way of communicating the disquiet of their daily reality to their church leaders and, if they did, were they listened to with respect? I don't know the answer to that. Perhaps they did. If so, it makes it harder to understand how a church leader could be making jocular remarks about the Führer when the Pope turned to him for guidance as late as March 1939.

We now know the story of one Catholic layman who tried to share the disquiet of his conscience with his bishop. Franz Jägerstätter, an Austrian peasant farmer, a married man with three small children, was executed by the Nazis in 1943 when he was thirty-six years old. He was put to death for steadfastly refusing to take the mandatory oath of unconditional obedience required of all those called to serve in Hitler's armed forces. He belonged to the village of St Radegund, where he was the sacristan of the little Catholic church. A priest of the same parish, Father Karobath, had been removed from his post because of his anti-Nazi views and it was he who later made known the heroic resistance of the young man and brought his ashes home from Brandenburg prison for proper burial. But at the time, when Franz Jägerstätter made his stand, he was told by his bishop that these were high matters of state, too big for him to comprehend, and that he should behave sensibly and join a war that was an anti-Communist crusade.

On 8 August 1993, the successor of that bishop, Maximilian Aichern, present Bishop of Linz, celebrated an open-air mass outside the Jägerstätter farmhouse with Franz's widow, children and grandchildren taking part. People from many countries of the world joined them to pay honour to that lonely peasant martyr through whom the Holy Spirit had sought to be heard. Who but the Spirit of God could have given him the insight and courage to do what he did and at the end to write from his prison cell, 'It is still best if I speak the truth even if it cost me my life'?

And in January 1995, at the fiftieth commemoration of the

liberation of Auschwitz concentration camp, the Catholic bishops of Germany as a body publicly admitted that the Catholic church had been partly responsible for the Holocaust, they deplored the lack of official and general protests by the church, they acknowledged that the church, too, had been tainted by anti-Semitism, and they asked forgiveness of the Jewish people.

The church has not always made a practice of humbly admitting where it has failed, so that plea for forgiveness was significant and full of hope. But the question remains. Did the Holy Spirit desert the German church in those years? Or did the German church desert the Holy Spirit? The bishops were striving to protect the church under a hostile regime. It was they who were making all the decisions. Cardinal Jozef Suenens of Belgium, speaking of co-responsibility within the church, remarked that 'it takes many to be intelligent'. But co-responsibility needs even more than intelligence, collective experience and expertise, valuable as these may be. It calls for a faith that really believes that the Spirit of God lives in every Christian and may choose to speak not just through the church leaders but through a peasant farmer from a remote village. The leaders of the church need to be open to such a possibility and must create structures where it can take place. And if, in the end, they are not sure where truth lies, they have the clear light of the Gospels and the wisdom of tradition to guide them.

15 Dilemma and Decision

Perhaps no event in the life of the church has demonstrated more clearly the need for true co-responsibility than the papal encyclical known as *Humanae Vitae* (Human Life), issued by Pope Paul VI in 1968. In it he condemned the use of contraceptives in the act of sexual intercourse in marriage. It seems to me, if there's one area where the church should listen most closely to the experience of its people, it is in the area of sexuality. And before Pope Paul VI wrote this encyclical it did look as though that was exactly what he was doing.

To help him in coming to a decision, in 1966 he established a commission that represented the whole church: lay people such as the American couple, Pat and Patty Crowley, who had founded the international Catholic Family Movement, theologians such as Bernhard Häring, cardinals such as the Archbishop of Westminster, John Heenan. The Crowleys saw to it that the voice of experience was heard at last. They brought with them their own research and they spoke from their own experience as a married couple with five children. They had a considerable impact on the proceedings. Here, it seemed, was the living acknowledgment that the Bishop of Rome, in union with all the bishops, can teach authentically in so far as they are all witnesses to the faith of the People of God.

The primary issue under debate was: should every act of sexual intercourse be seen primarily as a procreative act? Or was sexual intercourse a good and holy thing in itself as an act of love between a man and woman committed to each other in a solemn convenant? If that were the case, the couple themselves would be able to decide at what points in their marriage they would be open to having children. Implicit in this latter stance was the acceptance of contraception as a means of birth control. The commission was given the solemn responsibility of helping to discern what was nearest to the heart of God. It is important to remember here that all theology and teaching in the church come from four main sources: Scripture, tradition, experience and rational discourse. Since Scripture has nothing specific to say about contraception, and tradition has different mainstream opinions on the subject, it seemed that a well-grounded teaching would have to rely mainly on human and Christian wisdom, experience and discernment.

It was not until I read the writing of the highly respected moral theologian Bernhard Häring that I heard for the first time that there had, for centuries, been two mainstream opinions on birth control in the tradition of the church. Saint Augustine was the chief exponent of the belief that every act of intercourse must be primarily procreative. This was the view 'received' by the church and, as was its custom, it proposed this one viewpoint as the orthodox one and urged uniformity. But there were other views, and exponents of these included saints such as John Chrysostom and Alphonsus Liguori. Alphonsus took a strong stand in opposing the rigour of Augustine. He made his position clear when, in the eighteenth century, he wrote that, as an expression of the marriage covenant, intercourse between spouses is good and legitimate in itself, without any actual intention to transmit life being necessary.

In 1930, however, it was the Anglicans who really set the cat among the pigeons. At the Lambeth Conference of that year, after a long process of consultation and debate, they broke with the Augustinian tradition. They recommended the virtue and practice of continence as a noble way of family planning, but also considered that contraception was justified where necessary. Pope Pius XI reacted swiftly. He wrote an encyclical, *Casti Connubii*, in which he condemned contraception as a grave sin and a crime. As a result, the orthodox view was heavily underscored. But in 1930 the church was still operating within the monarchical model firmly established by Pope Pius IX some sixty years before, and the Pope would have been acting very much on his own in pronouncing this severe judgment.

It was different in 1966. At the Second Vatican Council a few years before, the monarchical model in the church had given way to the collegial one, and consultation with the College of Bishops, with the clergy and with the people was under way. It seemed that those, such as Cardinal John Henry Newman, who had always considered that the voice of the laity had a place in the formulation of church teaching were now being vindicated. So the Papal Commission had every reason to believe that Pope Paul VI would take their recommendations very seriously and it was with a high degree of confidence that the president and secretary presented their final report to him in person on 23 June 1966. The report recommended a change in church teaching on the subject and concluded by saying that the Catholic position on artificial contraception 'could not be sustained by reasoned argument'.

Before leaving the commission I think three events are worthy of reflection. Each throws its own particular light on the attitudes and outlook of the people involved. The first has to do with the rather quaint living arrangements for the married couples coming to Rome for the commission meetings: the wives were lodged at a convent while their husbands stayed at the Spanish College down the road! The second has to do with an interesting exchange between two commission members. When a priest member, a Spanish Jesuit, saw that the commission was moving in the direction of change, he asked in dismay, 'What then of the millions we have already sent to hell if these norms are not valid?' Patty Crowley is said to have looked at him across the table and replied, 'Father Zalba, do you really believe that God has carried out all your orders?'

The third point concerns a Polish cardinal who was appointed to the commission but chose not to attend any of its meetings. He was Karol Wojtyla, later to become Pope John

Paul II. I can't help wondering if his view on the nature of sexual intercourse and its meaning in marriage might have been developed further had he been exposed to those discussions. The proposition is not entirely improbable. Another cardinal, John Heenan, went to Rome as a very conservative prelate opposed to any idea of change. Yet in the course of those commission meetings where he heard the voice of the people most affected by this church law, he changed his mind on the matter and came to support change.

If Pope Paul was in any doubt of the views of the laity in general on what was now being called 'responsible parenthood', those doubts must have been dispelled in the following year when the Third World Congress of the Laity met in Rome in October 1967. This congress had been initiated by Pope John XXIII before he died, thus committing the Vatican and the papacy to inviting representatives of the laity from all over the world to express their views after the end of the Second Vatican Council. Accordingly, some 3000 men and women from every continent in the world converged on Rome. They came from Africa, Central America and the West Indies, Canada, the United States and Mexico, South America, Asia, Europe and Oceania (Australia, New Caledonia, New Guinea and New Zealand).

The Lay Congress was meeting at the same time as the Bishops' Synod, which brought representatives of the bishops of the world to Rome. It was a unique gathering of the church in one place and, one would have thought, an unparalleled opportunity for co-operation. But there was virtually no communication between the two. The main agenda for the Lay Congress was to explore the establishment of new structures that would enable the voice of the laity to be heard in the church at large and in their local churches. The congress itself was providing them with a structure, albeit a temporary one, where their voice could be heard in Rome itself. It was inevitable that they would turn their attention to the birth control issue, the most immediate and urgent topic for the laity at that time. Since the Papal Commission had given its recommendation to Paul VI the year before, there had been no word from the Pope, which indicated that he was still making his decision. Here was an opportunity for the laity of the world, gathered in Rome at his invitation, to debate the matter and give him their findings.

It has to be remembered that these were not the radicals from the ranks of the laity. Naturally enough, the delegation from each country was drawn from the lay organisations active at the time and established before Vatican II: the Saint Vincent de Paul Society, the Legion of Mary, the Catholic Women's League, the Apostleship of the Sea, all of them traditional church bodies. Any new blood was to be found in the representatives of such groups as the Catholic Family Movement and the Young Christian Workers. It puts me in mind of the Second Vatican Council itself, where almost every bishop, taken as an individual, could probably be considered conservative, and yet together they enacted the most sweeping changes that the church had ever known. Those who fear change have every right to be suspicious of bringing people together for discussion — it is always a dangerous exercise.

The recommendation that the Lay Congress submitted to the Pope was virtually the same as that already presented to him by his own commission. They asked that the church leave the choice of what means to use for achieving responsible parenthood to parents themselves, acting in accordance with their Christian faith and on the basis of medical and scientific consultation. Alarm bells began ringing all over Rome. Most of the lay delegates were about to have their first experience of the Roman machinery rolling into action.

The recommendation from the Third Lay Congress came to nothing. In his address Pope Paul reminded the delegates that their particular sphere of action was in the world and that church teaching was the particular sphere of the hierarchy. The congress responded by sending a delegation to the Synod of Bishops to press for greater lay participation at all levels of the church. The organising secretary reflected the delegates' frustration in a final address to the congress: 'to be able to play our part we must finally persuade the church hierarchy that we are with them, not as meek children, but as responsible collaborators. In the future, the laity must play the role, not only of fund raisers, but also of thinkers'. And all this happened nearly thirty years ago.

Pope Paul was to wait until July 1968 before making his decision. In the end he decided against any change. *Humanae Vitae* caused an outcry in the church without precedent in modern times. It was to no avail that the whole tone of Paul's encyclical was vastly different from that of his predecessor, Pius XI, thirty-eight years before. Where the one had expressed strong condemnation, the other showed compassion and pastoral concern. And where the language of 1930 was of uncompromising command, the voice of 1968 'invited the assent' of the faithful. Paul even went so far as to say, through his spokesman, Monsignor Lambruschini, that the norm given in his encyclical that 'every marriage act must remain open to the transmission of life' was neither an infallible declaration nor an irrevocable decision. It made little difference: the expectation had been too high and the wait too long. All that most people ever absorbed from that encyclical were the two words: no change.

In the ensuing ferment it was not immediately perceived that the debate had now expanded from the practice of sex to include the practice of authority. And if great numbers of the laity were upset by the denunciation of contraception and were concerned about its implications for their relationship with each other within marriage, many bishops were equally upset by the abandonment of the principle of collegiality and concerned about its impact on their relationship with the Pope in the exercise of authority within the church.

There has to be an explanation for Pope Paul's making a decision that did not take into account the recommendations of the commission he had called to advise him. Of course, his own personality and background played a major part. And one has only to read the story of his life written by the late Peter Hebblethwaite to get some idea of the pain of indecision that he suffered. But two years was a long time to keep people waiting. Anyone who knows what it's like to work with people in authority who can't make up their minds will understand. In my experience, it quite often happens that the person, after putting off a decision as long as possible and employing all sorts of stalling devices, will shock everyone with a sudden, sometimes inexplicable action. It's as though the burden becomes insupportable. There may have been something of this in Pope Paul's action. No one will ever really know.

Many other factors must have played a part. Perhaps he was so overwhelmed by the mass of information available to him that he considered it best to cut straight through it all with a clear direction to the church. He described himself at the time as 'submerged in a sea of documents'. Certainly he had the most up-to-date medical research at his disposal, much of it not widely known at the time. He was aware, for instance, that the contraceptive pill of nearly thirty years ago had the chemical potential to do grave harm to women's health. Paul's vision was always world oriented and it was a matter of deep concern to him that certain governments were already violating human rights by forcibly enforcing birth control, and in his words, 'claiming the power to intervene in the most personal and intimate responsibility of husband and wife'. It was only later that we became aware of what was happening in China, where women expecting their second child were made to have an abortion. And he knew of the degree to which powerful and rich Western nations were making a policy of birth control in poor countries a prerequisite for their receiving aid. But if Paul VI was viewing all the possible misuses of birth control on a global scale, that was not how millions of Catholic couples around the world were viewing it. They were simply waiting anxiously for the resolution of a question that was for them the 'most personal and intimate responsibility' of their lives.

Undoubtedly, Paul's difficulty was compounded by the problem that the church always faces when it must make a change of stance. It enfolds its decrees in such an aura of certainty that they seem to preclude any possibility of future change. So many things have been said with such authority that it becomes very difficult to admit that they might not be appropriate in another time. The church has a huge investment in always being right, and by suggesting that a former teaching needs changing, it fears that a shadow of doubt may be cast over its present proclamations. Pius XI had formally stated that contraception was a crime and gravely sinful. The young priest, Giovanni Battista Montini, later to become Paul VI, was working at the Secretariat of State at the Vatican when that encyclical was written. He knew Pius XI personally. It must have seemed inconceivable to him that, as Pope himself, he would change a papal teaching that had been issued in his own lifetime. He greatly feared that, by so doing, he might actually undermine the authority of the papacy itself. Unwittingly, that is what he did. It was a very real dilemma and its most obvious resolution was to place more trust in the wisdom, common sense and good faith of the women and men who make up the church.

Another element affecting Paul's decision was not apparent to the rank and file of the church because, of its very nature, it is hidden and secret. It is now known that he was under enormous pressure from certain members of the Roman Curia. A force to be reckoned with in the church, even by Popes, the Curia is the permanent bureaucracy of the Vatican — a type of civil service in which cardinals not only head each of its respective departments, known as congregations, but can also exercise influence in other departments. The result is an interlocking directorate of extremely powerful men.

The Roman Curia has never been at home with the concept of collegiality whereby all important decisions in the church are taken by the bishops with the Pope as their head. Such a system would seriously undermine the Curia's influence. They have always been unhappy at the prospect of becoming subordinate to bishops and they dislike the idea of bishops acquiring more discretion in governing their local churches. We are talking here about power, the kind of power that Jesus repudiated. And in this prodigious power game the Vatican bureaucrats enjoy the decided advantage of bureaucrats everywhere: that of being right there on the spot where policy is made. They are singularly unaccountable to the church as a whole. The bishops, by comparison, are scattered to the four corners of the world and are accountable in varying degrees to their people. And, paradoxically, whereas bishops are the successors of the Apostles, cardinals are, in the words of historian Gerard Noel, 'a dispensible invention of the eleventh century'. The college of cardinals could be abolished tomorrow, the college of bishops could not. Legitimate authority in the church belongs to them.

I have always been curious about the way the Vatican works, not just on the wider canvas that can be seen by everyone, but in its day-to-day life. I have never been to the Vatican State, that tiny nation of forty-four hectares, and I find it hard to imagine it. It came into being in 1929 with the signing of the Lateran Treaty between the Italian government and the Pope. It was devised by Mussolini to end the long feud that had been going on ever since 1870 when the Papal States and the city of Rome were forcibly incorporated into a united Italy. By this treaty the government recognised papal sovereignty within the Vatican State, and the Pope at last recognised the legitimacy of the state of Italy and renounced all claims to the former Papal States. The recognition of the Italian state meant that Catholics, after a political drought of half a century, could now licitly exercise their vote. It was one of Mussolini's most popular actions and one of the few that survived him, to be written into the constitution of Italy after the Second World War. It was also a very astute move on his part, placating the church at a time when he was consolidating his power and feared its opposition. For its part, the church was anxious to settle its long stand-off with the Italian state. (It is worth noting that one of the chief negotiators for this concordat between the Holy See and the kingdom of Italy was the distinguished diplomat, Cardinal Eugenio Pacelli, later to become Pope Pius XII.)

The Lateran Treaty gives to each succeeding Pope virtually all the legal rights of any secular head of state: diplomatic representation in other nation states, a place at international conferences, and a political right, over and above his spiritual one, to speak on world affairs. It explains why the Pope, on his overseas visits, has to be honoured as a head of state, and not just as the spiritual leader of Catholics within a particular country.

But what kind of life goes on within this tiny state day by day? When at last I was given that insight, I decided that I preferred not to know.

My discovery began when, in my local library, I came on a book called *A Thief in the Night*, by English writer John Cornwell. He was invited to write this book by a highly placed Vatican official, Archbishop John Foley, President of the Vatican Commission for Social Communications. Several books had already been published in which the death of Pope John Paul I on 29 September 1978 had been cast in a sinister light. The most damaging had been David Yallop's *In God's Name*. Because there had been an apparent cover-up of the events on the night of the Pope's death, Yallop was able to formulate the elaborate theory that, after only thirty-three days in office, Pope John Paul I had been murdered. In so doing, he had cast suspicion on certain people at the Vatican and horrified thousands of people around the world. Ten years after the event, rumours were still rife. They needed to be refuted.

Cornwell was given the job of unearthing the facts about what actually had happened and, so that he could do this, he was given rare access to life within the Vatican, which he recorded in almost diary form. People were advised to speak to him freely and he came and went virtually at will. I had never believed that Pope John Paul I was killed so it came as no surprise to find the claim refuted in Cornwell's book. But I was shocked by the picture he painted of the faceless men who inhabit that strange, male-dominated, celibate world so remote from any other experience of life. For the first time I could see how the cardinals of the Curia maintain their power and how vulnerable to their pressure Pope Paul VI could have been.

16 Nevertheless It Does Move

Something very significant happened after the publication of *Humanae Vitae*. Years before, Pope Pius XII had said that freely expressed public opinion was necessary for the health of the church. That is what happened now. The days of quiet acquiescence were gone. Christian Family Movements, marriage counsellors, therapists, theologians, pastoral workers, ordinary men and women all raised their voices in protest. Most significantly, bishops' conferences in various countries wrote their own statements allowing broad, pastoral interpretations of the Pope's encyclical. They were practising collegiality after the event, as it were.

But it didn't stop there. The alarm extended to the very highest echelons of the church, as has been revealed by what is now known as 'the secret of Essen'. This was a strictly secret meeting of five cardinals: Cardinal Julius Döpfner, Archbishop of Munich, Cardinal Bernard Alfrink of the Netherlands, Cardinal Franz König, Archbishop of Vienna, the English Cardinal John Carmel Heenan, Archbishop of Westminster, and Cardinal Leo Jozef Suenens of Belgium. This had never happened before, that five cardinals should meet secretly outside Rome. It was the measure of how shaken they were that Paul VI, after having given every indication that he would not announce important decisions without consulting the college of bishops, had quite unexpectedly come out with this encyclical denouncing artificial birth control. These five church leaders were deeply aware that the Pope's decision would cause a serious loss of credibility on the part of the church and a serious loss of authority on the part of the Pope.

The role of bishops, too, was made much more difficult by

the publication of *Humanae Vitae*. Those bishops' conferences of various countries, which gave their own interpretations of what the Pope had written on birth control, were taking on themselves full pastoral responsibility for the care of their own people. In the guidance that they now gave to the laity they were acting according to their collective conscience, even though it could appear that, in not quietly accepting and promoting the encyclical as it was written, they were challenging the Pope's decree and could even be accused of implicit disobedience to Rome. But bishops are well trained in church politics and in verbal gymnastics; they could protect themselves from such an accusation, while at the same time sending a message to their people that they did not support the absolutes of the papal decree. For those conferences of bishops who made this response, it was a remarkable precedent in modern times.

Although it would become apparent that a silent revolution was taking place in the church and that, in the process, the People of God were coming to a new spiritual maturity, the immediate results of the encyclical were far-reaching. Thousands of people simply left the church of their ancestors. And the haemorrhage has never been effectively staunched. Not all would have left because of the encyclical and no doubt some joined the exodus for other reasons. But for those people who left because they could not, in conscience, stay in a church whose official teaching they did not accept, it was a complex and anguished decision. In many ways, although it looked as though they were acting in a radical manner, they were just as likely to have been motivated by a deeply conservative belief system. What they seemed to be saying was that they had looked to the church not just to be the guide of but actually to *be* their conscience. And when they found the teaching of the church to be at variance with their own conscience, they felt they had no option but to leave.

Just like every other institution, the church operates out of a given time and culture. It was doing precisely that when it taught that the earth was the centre of the universe and the sun revolved around it. When, in the seventeenth century, Galileo put forward the teaching, based on new scientific evidence, that the opposite was the case, he was undermining the very base on which church teaching had been built. It was not surprising that the Inquisition condemned him. But where did that leave Galileo? As he rose from his knees before his judges, with the earth firmly back at the centre of the universe to everyone's satisfaction, he is supposed to have said under his breath, 'Nevertheless, it does move!' He had to rely on his own integrity and allow his own conscience to direct him to where he perceived the truth to lie.

And when, in the sixteenth century, Pope Leo X taught that the burning of heretics is pleasing to God, surely there were dissenting consciences, people disagreeing under their breath. And what of the various popes who justified and authorised slavery in their time? In my own lifetime, Pope Pius XI, in an encyclical at least as important as *Humanae Vitae*, claimed that co-education is erroneous and pernicious and against nature. That might have represented a fairly general belief at the time, but did every Catholic in 1929 agree? And if not, what became of them? Did they have no other option but to leave the church? They could stay — and probably did. But that does not imply that they were hypocritical. They could have recognised that, in all matters pertaining to their moral conduct, there is one authority higher than the church itself. And that is their own conscience.

There is nothing new about all this. It has always been the teaching of the Catholic church that, whereas the church is our objective guide in faith and morals, our conscience remains the final arbiter of our actions. But, although not deviating from this doctrine, the church has always appeared painfully inhibited about actually teaching it! I certainly haven't heard much enthusiastic endorsement of the place of my conscience in the moral order. I was far into adult life before I heard it spoken of in any way that could penetrate my consciousness and colour my actions. It's possible that some Catholics go right through life without ever hearing this fundamental truth and without ever embracing freely what their own conscience tells them to be right.

Their lack of confidence is understandable, when you come to think about it. Priests don't often preach in a reassuring way about conscience, bishops don't write pastoral letters about it and Popes don't write encyclicals about it. Whenever I have heard it mentioned it is always surrounded by so many cautions and qualifications and unmistakable votes of no confidence that the fundamental truth gets completely lost. Ah yes, of course, a person's conscience must be the final arbiter of his or her actions, but — and here the danger warnings inevitably begin — it has to be a well-ordered conscience, a well-informed conscience, a well-developed conscience, an educated conscience — every type of conscience, it seems to imply, except yours! And with every hedging qualification, the conviction is intensified that a lay conscience is not to be trusted.

I remember hearing someone say once, when speaking of John Henry Newman, the great English churchman who converted to Catholicism last century, that he always staunchly upheld the primacy of individual conscience, but was also completely loyal to the teaching authority of the church. It was said as though there were some inherent contradiction in his stance. That is simply not so. When Newman was upholding the primacy of a person's conscience, he was, by that very fact, being loyal to the teaching authority of the church. He was not denying that individual conscience stands in need of church teaching, based on Scripture, on centuries of tradition and experience and ministered by those whose authority is derived from that given by Jesus to his Apostles. Set beside such authority, our own conscience starts to look very frail indeed. In our more honest moments we have to admit that our judgments are often coloured by the demands of our ego and may have their source in the hidden wells of our own self-seeking. We certainly need the guidance of the church.

But the fact remains that there is a law written not in stone or in encyclicals, but in the human heart. And it, too, must be honoured and obeyed. When we find ourselves in legitimate disagreement with a specific teaching, or with the direction of a bishop or a pope for that matter, then the judgment call has to be left to the Highest Court of Appeal. Ask a Galileo or a Jagerstätter or a Mary MacKillop.

Cardinal Newman is dead over a hundred years now, but love and respect for him never seem to wane. The centenary of his death in 1990 brought an amazing outpouring of devotion from thousands of people, not least in New Zealand, and most of them lay people. I could never visit my brother Barry without hearing at least one reference to his best-loved churchman, a reference that often enough turned into a lengthy and loving dissertation! One of his favourite Newman quotes was: 'If I am obliged to bring religion into after-dinner toasts (which indeed does not seem quite the thing) I shall drink — to the Pope, if you please — but still to Conscience first and to the Pope afterwards'. And, Queen Victoria notwithstanding, he was wont to refer to conscience as 'His Majesty'.

For all that, it is not to Newman, but to another English cardinal of my own time, that I owe my deepest confirmation on this subject of the primacy of conscience. This came through an early experience of the communicative power of television. It was near the end of 1968. David Frost, at the height of his powers as a television interviewer, was speaking with Cardinal John Heenan, Archbishop of Westminster, on the subject of the Pope's recently published encyclical on birth control. I have taken the direct quotes given here from *The Anatomy of the Catholic Church* by the Hon. Gerard Noel, one-time editor of the English paper, the *Catholic Herald*. But I myself remember that interview as though it were yesterday — the thrust and parry of those two skilled and polished communicators, the interviewer asking one piercing question after another, pertinence without impertinence, and the churchman, courteous and couth, striving to answer each enquiry honestly without appearing disloyal to the Pope's decree.

In September of that year, Cardinal Heenan had said at a press conference that 'the priest is never bound to go against his conscience, but he is bound to make clear that the encyclical is the teaching of the Pope. He can then say as a matter of conscience that he does not agree with it.' Frost took up this matter of conscience, and little by little, step by inexorable step, we watched the cardinal being pushed to the wall. Finally the verbal fencing had to stop. The cardinal said, as the interview drew to a close, 'the teaching of the church is very clear. A man is bound to follow his conscience and this is true even if his conscience is in error.' Frost then put this question: 'And if they go to their priests and say that they're doing precisely that, what should the priest say?' Heenan replied: '"God bless you." If they're really following their conscience in the sight of God, which is all that matters — the priest, the bishop, the Pope doesn't matter compared with God.' So there it was. The leading churchman of England, seen and heard by millions of people, had just said something that, in my forty-six years as a Catholic, I had never heard explicitly stated before, not in the hundreds of lectures I had been given by priests in convent retreats and not in the hundreds of Sunday sermons I had listened to as an adult.

I think the church has paid a high price for this reticence. The church fulfils its vocation to teach and guide faithfully and lovingly. But it has not always been satisfied with that. Its teachers have often acted as though *they* were the consciences of their people, no doubt an easier role than helping others in the risky, difficult work of forming mature consciences of their own. Without the freedom to make their own judgments, and sometimes their own mistakes, people are in danger of remaining perpetually adolescent in their moral formation. And, at least until recently, that is what the church has done to its members. Some may see it as an excess of pastoral care, others as the work of a controlling patriarchy, but the fact remains that this exteriorising of conscience is very harmful to the Christian community.

If, in the past, Catholic people had received due acknowledgment of the dignity and authenticity of their own individual consciences, if they had been treated as mature adults, they might well be more ready today to seek the advice of their spiritual leaders — not with the intention of loading the responsibility on to them, but rather to receive guidance in taking responsibility for themselves. Sadly, many people who do not agree with the church's teaching on a particular issue are not ready to take advantage of its rich storehouse of grace, scholarship, wisdom and experience on any other matter. Many other people reject the church's authority altogether and go their separate ways. The numbers leaving the church are reaching massive proportions. And for people like me who love the church it is very hard to watch this happening.

It is very hard, also, to see what is happening to the loyal dissenters — those who remain in the church but can no longer give it unquestioning obedience. They feel, not without reason, that their opinions count for nothing. Added to this is their sorrow at seeing their children leaving the church that they themselves love, claiming that it has little or no relevance to their lives in the modern world. It grieves me to meet so many Catholics in this situation and to see the depth of their despondency and disillusionment. But I fear that nothing will change until the church begins to listen with greater respect and attentiveness to what the Holy Spirit of God is saying through its people. Only then will people begin to listen with greater respect and attentiveness to what the church is saying to them as it distils their experience into sound teaching.

A hidden price is being asked of people as they come to

terms with their freedom, a price that lies not so much in the moral as in the spiritual order. It is particularly sad because it concerns their relationship with God. As long as the church so strenuously condemns certain things that so many of its members do not, in their conscience, believe to be wrong, it creates a distance between great numbers of its people and itself that is very damaging to the relationship between them. It saps such precious things as loyalty to the church, trust in its dictates, respect for the advice of its ministers and, above all, the love that people would dearly like to give it as a teacher and a friend.

My first awareness of this spiritual hurt came from something said by a priest who has specialised in spiritual direction. It was his experience that people who sincerely act on their own conscience contrary to a church teaching, in distancing themselves from the church, also tend to distance themselves from God. In their prayer and inner life they deny themselves the closeness with God that they crave. They feel that they cannot afford to get too intimate with God. No matter what their conscience may tell them about the rightness of their position, the subtle conditioning passed on to them is too deep to ignore. Too often, there is a residue of unfounded guilt and the subconscious conviction that, when it comes to the crunch, God will side with the church.

In the meantime a profoundly significant development is still in process. People are increasingly aware that ultimately *Humanae Vitae* had as much to do with authority as it did with human life. Thousands of Catholics can now trace a watershed in their moral formation to around the year 1968. That was when they came to a new understanding of the role of their own conscience. As Peter Hebblethwaite notes in his book on Pope Paul VI, 'as a question for married Catholics, it was resolved by the primacy of conscience'. People who may never have heard of Cardinal Newman have come, by painful steps, to their own understanding that their conscience is the ultimate guide of their conduct. That this also happens to be the church's teaching on the subject may, sadly, still escape them. They are grounding their behaviour in the teaching of Jesus that we are, in the final analysis, to act with the freedom of a daughter or a son of God. He did it himself. He was faithfully obedient to the Jewish law and to its leaders in all things, except in those matters where his conscience told him they were wrong. Then he publicly disobeyed them and challenged them to change. He had to obey the law of God written on his heart before all else. And we have to do the same. It was in this, as in all else, that he came to set us free. But he paid a high price for his freedom of conscience and we should not expect to have it any different.

17 Looking Two Ways at Once

In the church today there is a growing tension between the teaching authority of the church and the authority of the individual conscience. The stress of this rests most heavily on the shoulders of those whose circumstances place them at odds with any official church teaching, but there is another group of people who, although not themselves at the interface of such tension, still find themselves caught in the balancing act it entails; they are the Catholic clergy in general, and the bishops in particular. These pastors have a binding responsibility to be loyal to the teaching of the church as ministered by the Pope and an equally binding responsibility to be loving carers of their people in all their difficulties and sorrows. Nowhere has this tension been more evident in recent times than in the question of Catholics who have divorced and remarried.

Although recent church teaching states explicitly that such people are not excommunicated by virtue of their remarriage — rather they 'are invited to its liturgies and to participate in parish life' — many Catholics in this situation are simply not aware of this. Some believe quite erroneously that, by virtue of their divorce alone, even though they have not remarried, they are somehow 'beyond the pale'. Because the church statements they have absorbed over a lifetime have been so absolute on the indissolubility of marriage and so uncompromising in their condemnation of divorce, they honestly believe that they are automatically excommunicated. And, sadder still, there are many more who, hurt by what they see as a lack of understanding by the church and in the face of the severity of its censure, have chosen to excommunicate themselves.

For those who stay there are painful limitations on their

inclusion in the life of the church. Because they are seen to be living in contradiction to the church's teaching on this matter, they are not permitted to receive Holy Communion. Now bishops and all other pastors know only too well that the implementation of this injunction is often pastorally harmful and can amount to a real injustice to certain members of their flock. In the light of this, several recent Conferences of Bishops have sought to counter this hurt by writing documents of their own in which they set out guidelines to help their people decide for themselves whether to receive Holy Communion, according to their own conscience. But this is not an easy exercise for the bishops concerned. One has only to read any one of these statements to perceive the tortuous path that they are treading.

Let us, for example, track the course taken by three German bishops representing the Upper Rhineland. In August 1993, they issued a pastoral letter on the care of the divorced and remarried that included guidelines on their admission to the reception of Holy Communion. In the light of the unprecedented interest their document generated outside their own region and far beyond Germany itself, the bishops were forced to point out that they had intended it solely for their own people. Nevertheless, they had unwittingly revealed just how urgently Catholics everywhere had been hoping for such a sign of pastoral care about this burning contemporary question. The people responded with gratitude and enthusiasm.

But bishops have to look two ways at once. When they looked away from the pastoral care of their people and turned their gaze towards Rome, they did not discern much gratitude or enthusiasm. On 14 September 1994 the Congregation for the Doctrine of the Faith issued a letter to all the bishops reiterating firmly that divorced Catholics who have remarried are not permitted to receive Holy Communion. So the three bishops felt it necessary to issue another statement, on 14 October 1994. It must have taken them nearly all of that intervening month to write such a document, so exquisitely poised was it between loyalty to Rome and loyalty to members of their local church. 'We wish therefore to emphasise explicitly that we do not find ourselves in any doctrinal disagreement with the position of the Congregation for the Doctrine of the Faith,' they wrote. 'The difference has to do with the question of pastoral practice in individual cases. According to the witnesses we cited from Church tradition, there does in the light of newer research, exist room beneath the threshold of the binding teaching, for pastoral flexibility in complex individual cases that is to be used responsibly. Such flexibility does not stand in contradiction to the indissolubility of marriage.' And so it went on, dense with loyalty, dense with care.

But the Rhineland bishops were not out on a limb in this matter. Several other bishops' conferences wrote their own directives to the people of their regions. In response to the Vatican document, the Belgian bishops told their people that they recognised 'that the Vatican document points out the traditional teaching of the Church, but as in other cases, the personal decision of the individual conscience is final'. And across the border in the Netherlands, Bishop Moeller of Groningen said in a radio interview that remarried divorcés should not be treated as 'lepers' and that the decision on whether to receive Communion rested 'completely and exclusively with the individual'. He added rather pointedly that Pope John Paul himself had said that the divorced and remarried were 'full members of the church'. And in Linz in Austria, once the diocese of Franz Jägerstätter, the pastoral council and the majority of priests have declared that they cannot put the Vatican veto into action.

The New Zealand Conference of Bishops, as is most often their wont, have remained silent on this question as it pertains to the reception of Holy Communion. It is not part of our culture always to want everything neat and tidy. Perhaps they simply trust their people to act with the spiritual maturity that the situation so obviously requires. Still, we must be grateful to those bishops who have grasped the nettle at last and taken the risk of wrestling respectfully with the centralised arm of the teaching church to search out a solution. It is a solution that has both to encompass the church's passionate desire to protect the institution of marriage and to recognise the pain and vulnerability of those who have not been able to sustain that ideal, and provide them with precious spiritual food when they are most in need of it.

The denial of Holy Communion, for whatever reason, is a very heavy burden to impose on members of the church. Only those who know what Communion means to them in their spiritual lives can have any idea of the pain of this loss. For me, it is epitomised in the memory of a Catholic man I knew years ago. I saw the intensity of suffering and the profound sense of deprivation that he experienced because he was denied Holy Communion, although for a quite different reason. He had married a non-Catholic and his wife refused to let their children attend a Catholic school. At that time, any Catholic whose children were not attending a Catholic school was in the same position as divorced and remarried Catholics are today: they were forbidden Holy Communion. This man had no option. If he took a stand on the matter his marriage would be broken. So, for the entire time that his children were attending a state school, he was denied what was for him 'the bread of life'. He came from a Catholic family with great faith and generations of commitment to the church. His brother was later to become a bishop. His own life was one of shining goodness. The pain of the penalty against him was indirectly imposed on his entire family.

When I come to think of it, I can't recall whether that particular law has ever been rescinded. But no one keeps it any more. Now, how could that have come about? Perhaps a handful of Catholics began to act on their own conscience in the matter and after a while the trickle became a flood. Finally, in the collective consciousness of all those who should have been living under this penalty, and equally in those who should have been imposing it, a spiritual consensus was arrived at unawares, and the law was quietly forgotten.

But the man I referred to earlier suffered his exclusion in an era when Catholics accepted each church law with unquestioning obedience, believing that not to do so was seriously sinful. These days I have only to go to Mass in any parish church in the city where I have lived for over fifty years to see how different things are now. In almost every case I see people who I know are divorced and remarried going freely to the altar. And I am aware that many people in that particular congregation know their circumstances and appear lovingly accepting of their situation. Otherwise they could hardly remain happily in that worshipping community. What the people of those communities are saying, implicitly and appropriately, is that the only people really equipped to assess the rightness or otherwise of their own situation are the individuals themselves. And that is what more and more of them are doing.

One of the bishops who believed that the 1994 Vatican directive should be absolute was Bishop Kurt Krenn of St Poelton in Austria. He reasoned that people who had divorced and remarried cannot receive Holy Communion because they live 'in continual contradiction to the teaching of the church'. But even he, when it was put to him, allowed that if their conscience told them this was not so, their decision must be respected. He did add a very significant rider, though: 'But the erring conscience cannot be elevated to the level of a doctrine'. Here was the heart of the matter, the potential danger the church perceives as it strives to maintain its part of this difficult balancing act. With that wonderful mix of wisdom and paradox that was his hallmark, G. K. Chesterton, in his book *Orthodoxy*, written early this century, put it this way:

> Remember that the Church went in specifically for dangerous ideas. . . . The idea of birth through a Holy Spirit, of the death

117

of a divine being, of the forgiveness of sins, or the fulfilment of prophecies, are ideas which, anyone can see, need but a touch to turn them into something blasphemous . . . If some small mistake were made in doctrine, huge blunders might be made in human happiness. A sentence phrased wrong about the nature of symbolism would have broken all the best statues in Europe. A slip in the definitions might stop all the dances; might wither all the Christmas trees or break all the Easter eggs. Doctrines had to be defined within strict limits, even in order that man might enjoy general human liberties. The Church had to be careful, if only that the world might be careless.

All of which makes good sense to me. But, for all that, my experience of practising Catholics in the church today does not suggest a people who experience much of the freedom of the dance and the grace to be careless.

18 Crisis of Obedience — Or Crisis of Authority?

M any of those who remain in the church, among whom I count myself, have made a long journey in the faith. From being passive receivers responding with uncritical acceptance to everything we were taught, we have become much more ready to examine, to appraise, to question, before giving unqualified assent to every one of its dictums. And this is healthy not only for us, but for the church of which we are an integral part. For the early part of my life I accepted, for instance, that it was a mortal sin to commit murder and a mortal sin wilfully to eat a meal of meat on Friday. In both cases equally, if I had not repented and confessed the sin, in the unfortunate event of my sudden demise I would go to Hell for all eternity. But it was not only nuns, trained as we were in docility of mind and will, who lived by such a belief system. Most adult Catholics, including those who were sophisticated and discriminating in their professional lives, ordered their spiritual and moral lives in unquestioning obedience to the teaching of the church. One Anglican historian suggested that Catholics were willing to pay a very big price for certainty in religion, so they could get on with their lives!

But changes were afoot even before the Second Vatican Council shone its light on such incongruities. One major work that had a considerable impact on me at the time was a massive piece of research done in the early 1960s by sociologists Andrew Greeley and Peter Rossi, whose findings were published under the title *The Education of Catholic Americans*. This showed that change was well under way among Catholics, even though the remnants of past attitudes were still visible. For instance, in answer to a question about the relative importance of love of neighbour as measured against eating meat on Friday, each different group answering the question registered over fifty per cent in favour of the church law. One commentator reasoned that this could very likely be explained by the fact that, whereas the Catechism always listed eating meat on Friday as a mortal sin, to be uncharitable could be classed as either venial or mortal! I recall a more informal questionnaire given to New Zealand secondary school pupils that offered the hypothetical Catholic dilemma of coming on an accident on the way to Sunday Mass. To stop and give help would mean missing Mass. What should they do? Now, what they actually would have done might well have been quite a different thing but, faced with the theoretical question, most wrote what they thought was right and said they would have to go to Mass. As the authors of the American survey observed wryly, it would not be the first time that structures had got in the way of the Sermon on the Mount. But it reveals the degree to which church laws were instilled at the expense of the law of love that Jesus so passionately commanded.

People with no memory of that era might ask how it could all have come about. They might even be tempted to say that I am exaggerating. Would that I were! But some of the explanation is to be found in the times in which we lived, where the prevailing climate affected society in general no less than the church. It was an era which accepted as inevitable and therefore legitimate that the lives of the many would be determined by the decisions of the few. In the world at large, white-skinned people controlled dark-skinned people as in our own backyard, where the Pakeha called all the shots for the tangata whenua. The rich controlled the poor, men controlled women, doctors controlled their patients, clerics controlled the laity. . . And, not satisfied with that, we religious took it a step further and committed ourselves by vow to lifelong obedience to the control of our superiors. All this was seen as legitimate because hierarchy was considered the natural, universal principle of all good social order, ordained by God 'himself'.

Books such as Greeley and Rossi's played a big part in our first nervous questioning of the absolute rightness of our beliefs and conduct. But for many Catholic New Zealanders of my vintage, one of the strongest catalysts to the exercise of our own God-given intelligence was one man — a Christchurch priest, brilliant in mind, dynamic in personality, fiercely articulate and utterly fearless in challenging the institution that he loved and despaired of at one and the same time. His name was John Curnow. Like every prophet of any age he was both loved and hated. He was motivated by a zeal for truth and possessed of what seemed to us a reckless courage. In the 1940s and 1950s he made us face up to those things in our Catholic lives that defied any intelligent explanation. He stripped us of our certainties. He questioned the church, grieving openly that it did not present a truer image of Jesus to the world. In some ways he was like Jesus himself, who wept over Jerusalem in love even as he prophesied that it would be destroyed through its own fault. John Curnow wrought havoc wherever he found himself, be it in the bishop's house, the presbytery dining room, the convent parlour, the living rooms of Catholic homes up and down the country. We watched with a mixture of apprehension and relief as one sacred cow after another was rounded up and unceremoniously slaughtered! After his death in 1991, people contributed to a book of reminiscences about him. It was aptly titled *When Comes Such Another?*

That was the beginning, but I have lived to see the ethos of those years repudiated at every level of society. People no longer believe that hierarchy is a divinely ordained order. Women, the poor, the laity, the Maori in Aotearoa New Zealand — group after group all around the world have, over the past three decades, asserted their right to be listened to in policy making. They no longer believe it is healthy, wise or even safe to let institutions rule their lives without question. And the failure of institutions, whether of church or state, to come to grips with this new expression of human dignity is the chief reason for the current decline in respect for authority. If institutions are no longer respected and obeyed, they have themselves to blame. Saint Augustine noted a very long time ago that every crisis of obedience is first of all a crisis of authority.

But there is one part of this phenomenon that institutions in general, and the contemporary Catholic church in particular, find very hard to bear, and that is that many of those who dissent remain its loyal members. And, significantly, these people never dispute the legitimacy of institutions as such, nor the existence of genuine authority, nor the need to love the church even as they criticise it. There is no doubt that they have plenty of precedent for their stance, both in the old order and in the new. They are walking in the footsteps of the prophets of ancient Israel who gave their first loyalty to God and, in so doing, often found themselves in loyal opposition to their religious leaders. Without its Isaiahs, its Micahs, its Jeremiahs, its Zechariahs, Israel would have been lost in darkness, straying far from Yahweh. The prophets loved Israel with loyalty and passion, but they were always a thorn in its side. They resisted the religious authorities to whom the community, including themselves, owed obedience. It was their love that motivated them to cry out and refuse to be silenced when they saw justice being violated, false gods being worshipped and any of God's people being oppressed by their leaders. And the more the prophets were repressed, the more persistent and penetrating were their cries.

Similarly, in the new order that he initiated, Jesus himself is a model of prophetic dissent. He not only cried out against injustice and oppression in his time, but openly broke the laws and traditions in which they were enshrined: he ignored obsolete laws about washing before eating, he healed on the Sabbath, he ate with sinners, he consorted with Samaritans, he spoke with pagans and healed at their request, he befriended lepers, he called women to be his disciples along with men. He was loyal to the Jewish religion and at the same time its fearless critic. And the Jewish leaders could not tolerate his dissent.

All of which brings me back at last to the man I went to see in Phoenix Park all those years ago, Karol Wojtyla, Pope John Paul II. His body has failed since that day in 1979 but the fire of his spirit is burning more fiercely than ever. He is a man of incomparable paradox: he has virtually no power as head of the Vatican state, yet he is the leader that no other head of state can afford to ignore; increasingly aged and frail, his towering personality dominates the church; at constant war with the world, he gives tender witness to his love for it; a philosopher, a poet, a dramatist, a linguist, an intellectual, he loves the pilgrimages and processions of popular religion with the simplicity of a peasant; a tough man of the people, he has no diplomatic or curial experience to complicate him.

I feel a range of complex emotions when I read what he says in different places and situations. I know how he suffered under Communist rule, but I hear him making the profound comment, in preparation for the Euro-Synod in 1993, that 'now that Communism has gone, we have to be on the side of the poor, otherwise they will go undefended'. Sometimes I hear him speaking of the human body as though it were the source of all evil, yet I know he would defend to the death the teaching of the church on the sacredness of matter, the sanctity of the body, the sacramental quality of our everyday lives, all made holy because God took a human body in the womb of a mortal woman. I hear him expressing great fears over the spread of fundamentalist religions in such places as South America and yet my ears ring with his silence in commending the base Christian communities that are the strongest expressions of the church in those countries. I hear his passionate appeals for peace and then I hear him half-regretting the loss of the ideological certainties that the divisions between Communism and capitalism provided. 'Paradoxically,' he said, '. . . the end of the bi-polar system has led to deep changes in the balance of world power. It arouses feelings of uncertainty and instability which sometimes nourish a certain regret for what was rightly called the balance of terror.'

That statement seems to reveal a deep-seated nostalgia for the blacks and whites of that recent past. And in his yearning that the church be wholly white, as he perceives that state, John Paul finds it hard to tolerate the various shades of grey that are an integral dimension of the human estate. No amount of repression will ever overcome that. Bans and silencing and rebuking will not avail. And the amazing thing is that Karol Wojtyla, of all people, seems to have forgotten that fundamental fact about the human condition. Perhaps the supreme paradox of his papacy is going to be that the man who, from his own experience, knows all about the harm done by repression under a totalitarian régime is, in his urgent desire to overcome the evil he sees on all sides, creating a totalitarian régime of his own. In every Catholic paper I open there are accounts of yet more papal bans and punishments and attempts at tighter control, be it theologians like Leonardo Boff, who has been silenced, ecclesiastics like Archbishop Weakland, who could not receive an honorary doctorate from a Catholic university that wished to honour him, or intellectuals like Teresa Berger, whom no Catholic university is permitted to employ, or be it the increasing practice of imposing bishops favoured by Rome on reluctant local churches.

Our knowledge of history, if not our own experience, tells us that the chief by-product of every repressive system is fear, and fear is the most destructive and paralysing of all emotions. John F. X. Harriott, who contributed over many years to the English *Tablet*, said it very well in 1989, not long before his death. 'Rome,' he wrote,

> cannot centralise power at the expense of neutering local Churches in closer touch with local realities. It cannot without

disaster, create bishops and other senior officials who are neither trusted nor respected by the people they are meant to inspire. It cannot publicly humiliate or disparage saints, prophets and pastors commanding the love and admiration of millions. It cannot silence its most thoughtful and respected theologians without inviting the belief that naked power rather than spiritual insight and pastoral concern is its chief preoccupation. A Church of craven bishops, cowed priests and listless people is a self-contradiction.

In the years since then, things have not changed and things have changed. Things have not changed in that the Roman appointment of bishops without due consultation continues, but things have changed in that there are significant signs that this practice will no longer go unchallenged. The listless Austrian giant has already been stirred to life. It took a scandal in high places, but it was the catalyst that was needed. The Archbishop of Vienna, Cardinal Grower, a papal appointee, was accused of having, twenty years earlier, sexually abused boys under his charge. The people looked to him to either deny or acknowledge these accusations. But he did neither. And the resulting outrage at his silence set rolling a wave of reaction that has swept up with it all the latent dissatisfaction with the church on every front. The petition that half a million Austrian Catholics have signed is not about Cardinal Grower. It is about openly discussing such things as optional celibacy for priests, the ordination of women and of married men and the process by which bishops are appointed with proper local consultation.

Things have not changed when the Vatican appoints a new archbishop in San Salvador, a man who is a member of Opus Dei, a right-wing movement in the church, and a former chaplain to the armed forces, the same armed forces that shot the beloved Archbishop Oscar Romero at the cathedral altar as he was saying Mass. But things *have* changed when the people bestir themselves, as the people of San Salvador did, to write to the Vatican expressing their concern, and warning that 'greater divisions, bewilderment, discontent, frustration and uneasiness' would be the outcome of such an appointment. In Ireland a bishop is called to Rome for asking that the subject of celibacy be opened to debate and priests and people inundate him with support. At the very time that a woman theologian in South America is silenced, the Pope writes a letter to women saying that their voice needs to be heard in the church. Women everywhere are expressing concern about what precisely that means.

19 I'm Sorry, Ladies, to Be So Late

The letter that Pope John Paul II wrote to women in 1995 was quite remarkable — remarkable because of its tone, and because it was written at all. Its tone was personal. I think every woman reading it was meant to see it as a letter written to her alone. A Pope apologising to women — that is the stuff of which history is made! In the light of the church's treatment of women over centuries, the letter has to be seen as an historical document. I, for one, never dreamed that I'd see it in my lifetime. One might have expected that women in the church everywhere would receive this extraordinary letter with unqualified delight. But it has caused scarcely a ripple; I have yet to come upon a Catholic woman who has read it. But maybe a cartoon in *Time* magazine at the time was saying something significant. It showed the Pope with his red cloak and long white cassock flying as he hurries up the path clutching a large bouquet of flowers. The caption read, 'I'm sorry, ladies, to be so late!'

I have always believed that a universal and unqualified apology, such as Pope John Paul II has given, was the only possible starting point for the church in its conversion of heart about women. At the very least, it would have to be a sincere acknowledgment of past wrongs and an appropriate expression of regret for its traditional attitudes. The overwhelming evidence of history is that, for centuries, the church has harboured an irrational fear of women. If we go back as far as Tertullian we read, 'The judgment of God upon your sex endures even today; and with it inevitably endures your position of criminal at the bar of justice. You are the gateway to the devil.' But what of Saint John Chrysostom, who said,

127

'Woman — a foe to friendship, an inescapable punishment, a necessary evil'? Or Saint Clement of Alexandria, who claimed, 'A woman should be covered with shame at the thought that she is a woman'? Or Saint Jerome, with characteristic bluntness, 'Women are the gate of hell'?

'A good Christian is bound, toward one and the same woman, to love the creature of God whom he desires to be transformed and renewed but to hate in her the corruptible and mortal conjugal connection, sexual intercourse and all that pertains to her as a wife.' That was Saint Augustine! But at least he sees us as creatures of God. Saint Thomas Aquinas, scholar that he was, couched his view of women in philosophical terms that were rather less flattering. 'As regards the individual nature, woman is defective and misbegotten. For the active power in the seed of the male tends to produce something like itself, perfect in masculinity; but the procreation of a female is the result either of the debility of the active power, of some unsuitability of the material or of some change effected by external influences. . . .' Nearer to our own day, G. K. Chesterton, who is now being tentatively promoted for canonisation, said expansively, 'There are only three things in the world that women do not understand and they are: Liberty, Equality and Fraternity.' To which one can only reply that since the first two have been systematically denied them and the third does not include them, it is little wonder that he finds their understanding defective.

These quotations are merely samplings from a mass of writings in similar vein, some of them vengeful in the extreme and not all of them, by any means, emanating from the church. But they still give us some idea of the awesomely perverted heritage that the church has to own in its attitude towards women, and they put the present Pope's apology at the end of the second millennium into some perspective. In his letter he acknowledges that the church has been conditioned by its history: 'In every time and place, this conditioning has been an obstacle to the progress of women. . . . This has prevented women from truly being themselves and it has resulted in a spiritual impoverishment of humanity.'

It has to be conceded that the quotations I have given come out of a social milieu very different from the one that prevails today, an environment where women were despised and feared in a male-dominated world. But there is little excuse for the church. It has always claimed that its environment is not that of this world. Rather, it was entrusted by its founder with an entirely new vision to give to the world.

It is hard to see how those saints I have quoted, if they were open to Scripture, could fail to acknowledge the profound respect with which Jesus treated women in his lifetime. We could excuse Saint Thomas Aquinas his ignorance of biology. After all, it was held for centuries that only the male seed was active in conception. The female was believed to make no contribution to such a noble enterprise. Her role was entirely passive; she simply provided the womb in which the foetus could grow. But we can hardly excuse him his lack of discernment of Scripture, where the love and respect that Jesus showed towards women are clearly revealed. When Saint Thomas was reading the Scriptures at Easter time, for instance, could he really have believed that Jesus' followers, chosen by him to be the first recipients of the glorious news of his resurrection, were nothing more than misbegotten and defective human beings?

When you read the Gospels with any degree of openness, it is abundantly clear that, even in a social climate utterly dismissive of women, Jesus treated them with equality and blessed them in a number of priestly tasks. The story of his encounter with the Samaritan woman at Jacob's Well has to be taken seriously. This person was despised on two counts: she was a Samaritan and she was a woman. In speaking to her at all, he was opening himself to severe religious and social condemnation. Yet he entered into a deep discussion with her. She was the first person to whom he revealed the theology of the mystical life he had come to impart to his followers and, having done that, he sent her to preach the gospel to others. In Bethany, he defended Mary in her formal assumption of discipleship. He made it clear to Martha, when she questioned her sister's behaviour, that Mary had a right to be sitting at his feet in the accepted stance of a rabbi's disciple.

At the house of Simon, where he was a guest at supper, Jesus lovingly accepted a woman who was a public sinner. But, more than that, he made it clear to his male companions, in the full face of their contempt, that she was behaving quite properly in anointing him. And he pre-empted any possibility of that particular incident being selectively overlooked by those recording the Gospels for posterity. Using his most formal and serious injunction, he said, 'I tell you solemnly, wherever this Good News is proclaimed, what she has done will be told also, in remembrance of her!' And later, after he rose from the dead, it was the women at the tomb whom Jesus commissioned to announce the amazing news of his resurrection to his male followers, and to the world. It should not surprise us that feminism has emerged with the greatest confidence in those nations whose past has been informed by the Christian story. It is the expression of what was unequivocal in the Gospel of Jesus Christ, namely that women are full and equal members of humankind.

It was fitting, then, that the Pope should turn our eyes to the Scriptures and call on the whole church to make the transformation that is urgently needed by modelling itself on Jesus Christ. He points out how Jesus 'transcended the established norms of his own culture and treated women with openness, respect, acceptance and tenderness'. It has to be noted that he also treated them with equality. But John Paul's letter goes on to proclaim the fundamental truth that, in doing this, Jesus 'honoured the dignity which women have always possessed according to God's plan'. Saint Paul was more explicit about what God's plan is. In his letter to the church in Galatia (3:28) he made it clear that women and men are equal in God's sight — 'in Christ, there is neither male nor female'. All are one in him. And in our own day, the Second Vatican Council, in its document *The Church in the Modern World*, reaffirms that same equality: 'any discrimination based on sex, race, colour, social conditions, language or religion, is contrary to God's intent'.

It's an interesting coincidence that, about the same time that the Pope made this public confession of the church's role in the oppression of women and apologised for it, the Southern Baptist church in the United States made a similar move. There are some significant analogies between the two. The Southern Baptists finally said publicly that slavery is sinful and asked forgiveness from blacks for the part the church played in their oppression. The traditional message preached from their pulpits had been that God had ordained the segregation of the races, so their statement, when it finally came, was a singular expression of conversion. Yet it, too, caused scarcely a ripple and the general consensus was that it had come too late. Too many African Americans had seen their church stand by while violence and injustice were perpetrated against them. Over the years the church had made no move to repudiate its traditional stand and to build a new theology of the equality of all people. As a result, it is losing its white American members and failing to evangelise the young. As its membership falls, it has come to realise that it needs the support of the African Americans, with whom it shares a strong belief in fundamentalism.

I believe that the Catholic church has come to a similar realisation about its own experience. It has never taken women seriously. Traditionally it has always seen them in terms of male-conceived stereotypes: they were either exalted as the saintly mother or the pure virgin at one end of the spectrum or condemned as the wicked temptress and seducer of men at the other. As the Pope honestly recognises in his letter, these attitudes 'have prevented women from being themselves'. The church has not accepted them as full-blooded human beings with the same quality, intelligence, attributes, strengths and weaknesses as men. And, therefore, it has not defended their claim to equal economic, political, social and religious rights. Like the African Americans, too many women have seen the church stand silently by. Women have been the backbone of membership of the Catholic church and it is now losing them in significant numbers. And it, too, is failing to evangelise the young. In Rome, as in Atlanta, the message is being received.

One leading African American said that the Southern Baptist church's change of heart has come at least a generation late. It would have made a significant difference to African Americans, to the course of American history and to the future of the church itself, if the church had made its commitment to justice when the blacks were at the height of their struggle thirty years ago. The lone voice of Martin Luther King begged them to do so, but they let the opportunity pass them by.

There is a striking similarity here again with the attitude of the Catholic church towards women. Thirty years ago, leading feminists were saying all the things that Pope John Paul is saying in his 1995 letter. He has taken up all their demands: equal pay for equal work, justice and equality in conditions of work, justice for working mothers and women in the home, fairness in career advancement, equality of spouses with regard to family rights. It is very encouraging to hear all this being said so clearly by the head of the Catholic church and nearly every woman who has been asked to comment publicly on his letter has expressed her pleasure and gratitude. But each one has also noted that, although he asks that women be granted equality with men in all walks of life, it is in the world that these ideals are to be sought. He does not speak of equality and leadership for women within the church.

In one of the most significant aspects of his letter, the Pope calls for legislation to constrain the widespread violence against and the sexual abuse of women and, in doing so, he breaks the long silence of the church about this dreadful scandal in society. He writes feelingly of its 'long and degrading history, albeit often an underground history'. And he adds this important rider: 'It is a crime for which guilt needs to be attributed to men and to the complicity of the general social environment'. When feminists say that, even today, they are often accused of being anti-male. Don't we know that women often bring it on themselves? But what a difference it would have made if the church had spoken out against these injustices thirty years ago. Or even twenty. Or even ten.

It was too much to expect, I know, but I can't help grieving over the good that could have been effected and feeling a profound regret for the ground that the church has lost. But if the official church remained silent, individuals within the church did not. We have had our own Martin Luther Kings. When I began writing this I went to my collection of cuttings filed under 'Women'. I scarcely expected to find anything of use there, because the file consists of an old box in a shed and the filing process itself has long been abandoned, along with the optimism with which it was begun. So I was intrigued to find an article printed in 1975 in the Catholic paper that used to be called *Zealandia*. It was written by Father Tissa Balasuriya, who was visiting this country from the Philippines. In reflecting on women's equality, he pointed out that what was normal in the time of the Jews and the Romans cannot be regarded as universally valid, particularly today when we have women prime ministers, legislators, climbers of Everest, astronauts and physicists, and women active in every other field of scholarship and endeavour. He drew from that the logical conclusion that there was scarcely anything in the ecclesiastical offices that a woman could not perform and he concluded, in reference to Indira Gandhi, who was then Prime Minister of India, 'A woman is capable of being Prime Minister of the world's largest democracy. There is no reason why she cannot look after a diocese.' That was written twenty years ago. Anyone could be forgiven for thinking that we haven't come very far.

20 She Looks Like Christ

B ut things are seldom what they seem. Very significant advances have been made in the last few decades. More and more women are becoming highly qualified in fields that were formerly the preserve of men, and most often of clerics. Women are becoming theologians, Scripture scholars, church historians, liturgists and spiritual directors. And, most important, these women are writing — and from a woman's point of view. Of its very nature it is subversive literature. They are writing with such energy and power because they are turning over new, fresh soil: they are finding a new language for new concepts, conceiving creative ways of worship that spring from the female understanding, devising alternatives to old, worn-out ways of doing things, emphasising relationships in the church, seeing God in new ways that inspire new ways of praying. What they are writing could come only from the hearts and minds of women. And other women are reading what they write and, for the first time, experiencing history, Scripture, theology, liturgy and spiritual direction from a feminine perspective. No one can describe the excitement of this — it's new wine!

There is a marvellous irony in all of this. If the services of this new breed of female scholars were being used more fully in the church at the local, the national and even the international level, if the male church were not so threatened by them, so afraid, then these women would probably not have the energy or the time to write so prolifically. But, as it is, they have all these qualifications and nowhere much to take them. So they are turning to their pens and pouring out ever-increasing numbers of books, articles for Catholic magazines and secular periodicals and tapes for study groups to supply an insatiable market of women readers. And consciously or unconsciously, many women are beginning to read only those books that have been written by women. It is an interesting state of affairs and most likely a transient one, give or take a generation or two.

In my walk of life I meet few of these high-powered women. But I meet a considerable number of ordinary women like myself who make up the rank and file of women in society and in the church. And it is among these women that significant changes of outlook are taking place. I have been noting this for the past two decades. My benchmark, 1975, was International Women's Year and, to mark it, a national conference of women was held in Wellington. Two years later there was another one in Christchurch. Members of our community attended both. In the main, these conferences attracted middle-class women who were already interested in the women's movement. At the time, we made a considerable effort to interest other women in the Christchurch conference, but without much success. Most of them were simply not interested. And the word 'feminist' terrified them. But in the intervening twenty years that has changed. Today, we would have no difficulty at all in interesting women in a similar conference. Ideas that two decades ago were current only among a small élite are percolating merrily through the whole body. One of my favourite interior chuckles over the years has been to hear a woman saying, 'I'm not one of those feminists, but . . .' as she goes on to propound a classic feminist principle!

If any evidence were needed of the way that the woman on the street or the woman in the pew is changing, we had it in Christchurch recently. The occasion was an ordinary Sunday morning where people were sitting at Mass. Anyone observing the womenfolk that day, saying their prayers, keeping half an eye on their children, ready to listen attentively to the homily in the hope of spiritual nourishment in their demanding lives, would scarcely have seen them as potential rebels. But things were to be a little different that day. There were no fewer than three letters waiting for them. One was from the Pope, telling them that they could never be priests in the Catholic church; the second was from the College of Bishops of Aotearoa New Zealand, and the third was from their own bishop. All said in effect that there was to be no further discussion on the matter. Now, my guess is that if all this had happened twenty years ago, only the merest handful of women would have been outraged. But in 1995 the reaction was something akin to spontaneous combustion!

In some churches, women walked out, feeling that they had been insulted as adult human beings. Many sat in shocked disbelief. And a few, following a long tradition of the oppressed when roused, went on to organise. They formed a body called Catholic Women Knowing Our Place, providing an ongoing forum for women to reflect on their place in the church, to pray and study together, to experience solidarity and to consider strategies for the future.

It is a remarkable phenomenon of this era that so many Catholic women are experiencing a call to the ordained priesthood. Women talk openly of this clear conviction that they are being called by God to be priests. For many years, women in other denominations have experienced this call, and have been ordained as priests in their respective churches, but it is only in the last decade that significant numbers of Catholic women have had the experience of this calling. Only a church that has shown systematic disregard for women's experience could ignore what these women are describing. What we are seeing here is a sign of the times that requires serious discernment, not dismissive condemnation. The old language of denunciation and ban is no longer appropriate.

I do not believe that this call to ordained priesthood is the outcome of seeing women ordained by other churches. It does not stem from an outside influence. It has its source deep within the church itself. It is rooted in the theology of the

Second Vatican Council, which rediscovered and restated the teaching of the church on the true significance of the sacrament of Baptism. It is through Baptism that the Holy Spirit is present in the whole People of God, in women and men alike. As a natural expression of this, the church has called on all lay people to practise their baptismal priesthood in many forms of service. This means that women now read the Scriptures to the congregation at Mass and distribute Holy Communion. On behalf of the parish community, they prepare people who want to become Catholics for their entrance into the church; they organise programmes of preparation for the sacraments of Baptism and Confirmation, Eucharist and Reconciliation; they work with couples preparing for marriage and they minister to the sick and dying. In some places where there is no priest, or where he is too old or overworked, they give Benediction and lead the traditional Lenten liturgy of the Stations of the Cross. In isolated cases they are running parishes and the priest comes only on certain Sundays to say Mass. The Catholic people are now well accustomed to seeing women taking places of leadership in their community. And, as more women come to exercise this form of priesthood, many are perceiving a call from God to the ordained priesthood. The Holy Spirit blows where it will and the Spirit of God is to be trusted.

This development within the church is wider than women. It is a call to the proper empowerment of all baptised believers, among whom ordained leaders, both men and women, will serve the church community. In the meantime all official leadership and power is vested in the narrow model of the ordained celibate male. And in the meantime, too, we have the situation where, because of the shortage of priests, whole Catholic populations in such places as South America are for months on end deprived of the inestimable grace of the Eucharist. This is because the church will not ordain any of its married members. It is strange that a church law is thereby given priority over the spiritual needs of thousands of its members. We are asked to accept that, because Jesus was a celibate male, every ordained priest must be celibate and male. If we take such literalism to its logical conclusion, then every priest should be a circumcised Jew.

In the end, it is the work of God that is done at the altar. Since the Second Vatican Council, we now perceive the church primarily as a community of people who, through their Baptism, have received a universal call to holiness. Nowhere is the church more real and visible than when it is gathered for Sunday Mass. The priest is there in a twofold role: to represent the community before God and to represent Christ to the community. But the community is made up of women as well as men. Representation really matters. Women never have the experience of seeing themselves at the altar representing the community before God. And the community never sees God reflected back to them in female form, representing all that is feminine in God. It is an abiding loss at many levels. Not the least of these concerns our perception of God, who is neither male nor female, but embraces something of both in a divine being.

In 1994, when Pope John Paul II made his historic visit to Denver in the United States, 186,000 young people from all over the world came to meet him there. It was a wonderful encounter. One of the most beautiful liturgies celebrated on that unique occasion was a Stations of the Cross held on a glorious summer's evening. Each station marked an event in Christ's Passion: his betrayal by Judas, his judgment at the hands of Pontius Pilate, his denial by Peter, his scourging, his being crowned with thorns, his crucifixion, his promise to the good thief, his last tender words to his mother Mary and to his disciple John, the two people that he loved most dearly. At each station those thousands of young people bowed their heads in reverent silence for meditation and prayer. It was a deeply moving occasion. But there was one aspect of this sacred drama, profoundly beautiful and bittersweet, that made the biggest impression on those who were there: the part of Jesus Christ was played by a woman. She was Christina Brown, twenty-three, sloe-eyed, olive-skinned, long crinkly hair parted in the middle. In an interview later, the priest responsible for the liturgy, Dan Anderson of Cincinnati, said simply, 'She looks like Christ.' And the director of the Vatican press office, Joaquin Navarro-Valls, took it further. 'A woman can represent all humanity,' he said, 'and all humanity was represented by the death of Christ.' It seems so simple: if a woman can represent all humanity, it is hard to see why she cannot be a priest.

Those who are called on to explain these things do not have an easy job. Until recently, girls were prohibited from being altar servers. In 1994 the church lifted this prohibition. But a few years before that, in answer to a letter questioning this exclusion, Virgilio Noe, now a cardinal, wrote that the reasons why females could not serve on the altar had their source in 'Scripture and tradition, liturgical principles and practice, sacramental theology and ecclesiology'. It's hard not to notice that these are all now cited as reasons against the ordination of women! This letter went on to say, 'In any case, the church has the authority to . . . assign the various roles performed in these celebrations.' That is nearer the heart of the matter. I think it would have been easier for him, and more acceptable to his enquirer, if he had said simply, 'The church doesn't want girls to be altar servers.'

I know of no fewer than three Catholic women who have received the call to ordained priesthood and are acting on it. They have been nurtured in Catholic homes, two of them in Catholic schools and one through the fullest adult participation in a Catholic parish. But they have decided not to wait. None is known to the other, yet each has converted to the Anglican church and is seeking ordination. Every church is in need of reform, especially in its relationship with women. Those women who have joined the clergy of other denominations are obviously prepared to work for that reform from a position of power within their church. Reform in those churches could be largely the fruit of women's influence, acting from within the clerical state. But as the Catholic church moves slowly along the path of change, women who choose to remain its members must play their part, for the time being, from outside the clergy. And the ordination of women might come as the result of its transformed life. It might prove to be the fruit, the culmination, the peak of its reform. In some ways, given the present solitary life of the Catholic cleric, this may be the more attractive alternative for women. But it is also the more dangerous for the church, given the number of women who are leaving because they can see no hope of change. I grieve for their going because we need them.

Conclusion

I am not the same person who, as a tired pilgrim, boarded the boat at Mull on a dull, overcast afternoon to cross the water into the strange and beautiful light of Iona; nor am I the same person as the reluctant 'missionary' who drove across the border into the war zone of Ulster; nor the excited visitor who walked before dawn along the canal in Dublin to welcome the Pope to Ireland. But those events in that 1979 journey have been woven into my own life journey and remain an integral part of it.

I do not know if life at the abbey on Iona flows along as it did during our visit, although I'd be surprised if it does not. But pilgrims from all over the world will still be making their way there, of that I'm certain, and the island will have lost none of its mystical quality, its sense of timelessness, its tangible relationship with a sacred past. It will always be holy ground.

I rejoice that the yearning for unity and peace that Donald Malloch and I encountered that day in Lurgan, in people from both sides of the conflict, is at last being honoured by those in authority and is being patiently moulded into a reality in the present peace talks. Both the Matthews and the Brady families are now going about their daily lives with a new sense of freedom and safety and with hearts full of hope for the future.

Pope John Paul II has grown old in the years since I and a million others gathered in Phoenix Park to welcome him. But he has lost none of his passionate desire to save the soul of the world and he challenges injustice with all the fiery courage and stamina of a young man. His directions to the church itself are as clear and unequivocal as ever. But the women and men who are its members are now asking not just for a strong voice but for a listening ear. Church leaders will need to take them seriously. I believe that, for the tree of the church, they are the scent of water of which Job spoke so long ago:

> Though its root grow old in the ground,
> yet at the scent of water, it will bud
> and put forth branches like a young plant.